i am jess

---

a memoir

Jessica Fahl

Make a wish...

Contents

The Beginning of the End

S itting on the floor of our home office, I was surrounded by paperwork; piles of bills and credit card receipts closed me in, suffocating me. Scott kept everything, every piece of mail that came to the house. I disliked clutter and it had always annoyed me that he kept stacks of paperwork around the house. But now, I was grateful for the opportunity to sift through them, to find information.

I was astounded at the things I found and became obsessed with reading through them, finding more and more outrageous line-item purchases; expensive dinners and shopping trips in Vegas, nail salons, custom-designed clothing, porn sites, and donations to websites for women that wanted breast implants. He was living this extravagant lifestyle away from home while his postpartum wife stayed home to care for their newborn and their special needs child; he had no regard for any of it.

All of this information should have sent me running, taking the boys, and leaving. But I stayed. I stayed because I was too broken to leave. Because I didn't know where I would go or what I would do. I waited until he came home the next day to confront him about what I had found, my stomach aching from the knots tied so tightly within it. I tried to remain calm.

"You're disgusting. You have an entirely different life in your mind than you have here with us. "

Scott started laughing, asking, "What in the hell are you talking about, psycho?"

"I've been going through the office computer and paperwork and you're obsessed with porn and sex!" fighting my urge to break down sobbing, I started yelling, angrily.

"And you're paying *other* women to get their *boobs* done? There's sex and porn everywhere, and *obviously*, you haven't *really* been traveling for work with all those receipts from Vegas…"

I didn't know what more to say as there was nothing he could do to deny it, and I didn't care much to hear him explain it anyway. As was typical, he deflected, and I became the one with the problem. Suddenly, I was a stalker invading his privacy, and *that's what I get* for going looking through things that aren't mine. What did I expect of a husband that wasn't getting as much sex from his wife as he wanted? Not an ounce of remorse, not a single attempt at an apology, and not a single acknowledgment of the pain he had caused me.

Every time I tried to catch him in his lies, he'd accuse me of being a stalker and that I was crazy. I did feel insane! The absolute denial and refusal to validate any of my concerns was the cruelest form of manipulation I faced. Every time I'd find something new, I'd think, "There's no way he can deny or get his way out of this one." I didn't know how this could be happening, how someone that I thought loved me could treat me this way, with such disregard.

This terrible information I'd learned was all my fault because I went looking for something I had no idea I'd find. Broken and defeated, I left the topic alone and went on with daily life as usual.

Telling this part of my story screams "How could you not

leave?!" This scene in a movie would be when the wife tells her husband to leave, to get out of the house and she doesn't care where he goes. Those women are the strong women, the ones that have been betrayed and won't stand for it. Those women have this horrible thing done to them just once and they say, "No more, not ever again." I am not a member of that group of women. I am a woman who was so worn down from years of emotional neglect and abuse that I was used to it.

I am not special. I have done nothing extraordinary, and nothing extraordinary has happened to me. I'm telling my story as if it were to a close friend sitting next to me on the couch with a glass of wine, because friends help each other, and I need more friends. I need friends to know that their stories are important enough to share. How you experience something is valid, and even if you don't feel like your something is significant enough to matter to anyone else, find people that will listen. A lot of people know someone that has gone through an unimaginable tribulation. Their reaction and response will not be the same as anyone else's, but the more stories we hear, the more we can try to sympathize with others and learn to show compassion.

My story is about falling in love with a man I thought loved me, only to find out I'd been emotionally manipulated for years. It's about realizing afterward that I'd been completely isolated from the truth, not knowing what it meant to be loved. Once the fog began to clear, I found happiness in myself and now have a life I am proud to call my own. My story is about "things" that I've gone through in my adult life, which there are quite a lot of given that I've only been an adult for like, 5 years... totally kidding, I'm old. Listening to others' stories helped me realize I wasn't alone, and I want others to know they're not alone either.

My story is worth telling, even if it's only to release the pain and sorrow I hold in my soul. I want to share my experiences in hopes that I may reach another that is suffering without knowing they're suffering, to let them know the world is a very bright place and they deserve all the happiness they dream of.

Before Him

I am the oldest of four daughters, and I exude all the quirks and characteristics of typical first-born children. I am reliable and mature, a caretaker, and I aim to please; I'm organized, ambitious, and very type-A. My sisters typically fall into their respective birth order traits as well, being middle, middle, and youngest. As the oldest and bearer of the "dependent on others' approval" trait, I followed the traditional path after high school – college, wedding, job, babies, etc. My sisters have traveled along different paths, taking their time in deciding what they want to do when they grow up, experiencing all that life has to offer. I've been jealous of them throughout the years, wondering what my life would've looked like had I been less rigid in the goals I'd set for myself, less anxious to get my life "started."

There are nearly nine years to the day between my youngest sister and me, and we have not traveled along the same path in the slightest. None of us have. Most people that know us would say that they have never seen sisters so different from one another. Even though we all grew up in the same house and came from the same parents, we are all apples that fell from long branches off the tree in opposing directions: North, East, West and South.

Growing up we weren't remarkably close as sisters often are. I have numerous friends and acquaintances that have one or more sisters, and they all seem to be the best of friends as adults. They get together often, and their kids are not only cousins but the best of friends, too. I've been jealous of them, too.

We spent a lot of time together when we were young. Our parents took us camping, on annual spring break trips to Florida, and tried to have family dinners at least three to four nights per week. There were "green bean races" at dinner, where we would see who could eat a green bean the fastest. Somehow, daughter number two (in birth order only!), Marie, always won. She almost didn't even have to chew them, just opened and down the hatch it went!

As I was the first child for my parents, I was special. For nearly three whole years, I was the only one to be cared for, doted on, and loved. Dad had always wanted kids, several of them, but Mom wasn't so sure. They both came from families of four kids, my dad the oldest of four boys, and my mom the youngest (by far) with two sisters and one brother. Apparently, four was the number of kids to have!

When I was born, Dad was in his residency for medical school, and Mom wanted to be a career woman. Her first love was biology, and as a self-proclaimed science nerd, she tested out of all the intro courses in college. Her oldest sister used to take her out fossil hunting, so she decided to pursue geology, graduating with two bachelor's degrees – geology and geological engineering. Mom didn't set goals for herself, she went with the flow and dealt with situations as they arose. She never thought she wanted children yet ended up with four of them because Dad kept wanting more. When Mom was pregnant with her fourth daughter, my youngest sister, the doctor remarked that she must be trying for a boy, which upset her tremendously; she loved her children, regardless of their gender, and wasn't accumulating children in the hopes that one of them might be a boy. She made sure we had a pantry full of snacks for after school and carted us around to our sports events. She bought me my first car, a white Oldsmobile Toronado with a red velvet interior. She found it at an auction, deciding it was a safe "boat of a car" and great for a first-time driver. Mom was a helper and a fixer and wanted to help others fix things, like their taxes or purchasing a home, and she's great at it.

Dad was a nature-lover and has been outside more often than in for as long as I can remember. He would go for a run outside for an hour or two every day, even in the dead of winter where snot and tears would freeze on his facemask and it looked like he'd just taken a face plant into the snow. He was once on the cover of a running magazine. The picture was of him running through the snow, passing by the crooked, old red barn at the end of our hobby farm driveway. As kids, we were so proud of our dad and thought it was so cool that his picture was on the cover of a magazine.

We lived on twenty-five acres with a lot of lawn to be mowed. When we first moved into that house, I was eleven, and Dad used a push mower to mow the lawn. Not a gas-powered push mower that didn't have a self-propelled option, an actual non-motorized mower consisting of five long blades with wheels on either side attached to a handle that you pushed around while it clipped the grass. After about a year he realized this wasn't efficient and wasn't feasible for his young daughters to use, so he bought a gas push-mower that we could use to help with the lawn. I would argue that a lot of people with a lawn this size would have a riding lawn mower, but not my dad. He wanted the exercise and effort of doing work. In addition to the hour or two runs every day, he spent just as much time fiddling in the garden (both vegetable and flower), mending the fence, or pruning bushes and trees. His second full-time job was the farm's caretaker.

Dad's true full-time career was as a doctor, a family physician. He graduated with honors from medical school the year I was born; undertaking his residency while I was a toddler. I think he was meant to be a doctor, and he loved his patients. He specialized in family medicine because he enjoyed caring for all ages and wanted to be able to address any ailments they had. His patients became regulars and we often knew their stories by first name, even though we never met any of them. Having a dad as a doctor meant that kids at school thought we were rich, and friends often teased us about our "huge" house and how much money we must've had. I didn't feel rich, and I didn't feel like we were different from any other family. I often said "My *parents* have money!" and it wasn't *me* that was the different one. Dad wanted the big house, the farm, and the nice things, and Mom managed the finances to make those things happen for him.

Looking back on my childhood and my relationship with Dad, there are only big moment memories or memories evoked from photographs. His true loves were his career and his outdoor hobbies, and sometimes those things would intertwine with us, if we'd be outside playing catch or riding bikes, or when we'd go camping as a family.

Two days a week Dad had to work the evening shift at the clinic, so on Thursday nights Mom ordered pizza and we watched *Friends*. We lived on a hobby farm across from a lake with a beach; there were a lot of animals to take care of and a lot of space to roam. We had goats, chickens, horses, dogs, and a cat. I liked the horses but hated the chickens—mostly the roosters. They would chase after us whenever we'd go down to the barn, and they terrified me. Tiny creatures that I'm sure I could've launched across the yard with a swift kick, but instead, I just tip-toed by to not disturb them.

Mom sent Marie and me to horse camp a couple of years in a row, so we learned how to properly ride them and take care of the tackle. We had a couple of big ol' Clydesdales, like the Budweiser horses, named Bob and Blossom, and our parents would hook them up to a trailer so we could go for hayrides around the neighborhood. During one of those hayrides, whoever was "driving" the horses dropped the reins, and I remember jumping off the trailer, running up to the horses, and grabbing the bridle and reins to get the horses to stop again. Clearly, they couldn't have been running, or even trotting, if I was able to catch up to them, but somehow, I remember "saving the day" by getting them to stop so we could continue the hayride. People called me brave, but I didn't feel that being brave was one of my personality traits; I simply did what needed to be done in the moment.

At ten years old I was babysitting the neighborhood kids, sometimes three at a time. I had three younger sisters, two of them under two at the time, so I was used to helping out at home. By age twelve a friend and I started a day camp for the neighborhood kids called "Sunny Day Camp." We were just kids ourselves but were bored and ambitious. We printed flyers and dropped them off at the houses we knew had kids, and almost all of them signed up. For a few hours every day for a week, the backyard was filled with fifteen kids playing games or doing some sort of arts and crafts project. I'm sure we could've made a real business out of it as the years went by, but we mostly did it just for fun and something to do. My goals then were to be a teacher and a mom when I grew up because I loved being a caretaker and hanging out with kids.

In elementary and middle school, I always felt shy and uncomfortable around boys, which I thought was because I didn't have brothers from whom I could learn about boys. My friends didn't seem to have the same insecurities, which made me feel even more awkward in my own skin. By the time I reached high school, I must've figured it out because some of my closest friends were guys. With them, there was no drama and things just seemed easy. They didn't take hours getting dressed up to go out or gossip about what other people were or weren't doing.

"Want to come over and hang out?" meant exactly that – let's listen to some music or watch a movie and have some popcorn. I remember lying on the couch watching movies with Matt, the big, hairy, hockey player that everyone called a teddy bear. Just the two of us, not talking about much, but enjoying each other's company. There was nothing romantic about it; we were truly just friends.

I'd stay up late with my friend Eric at whoever's party we were at, just chatting about life and who was going to do what after high school. Eric was a grade above me in school and had been dating one of my girlfriends for a while. He was genuine in his friendships, making sure everyone was comfortable and having a good time. He was kind and caring, the quiet yet hilarious type.

I often drove around town with my friends Bobby and Dan, and they'd play me all kinds of new music they had found. We'd lie on the floor in the living room, the three of us in a row with the speaker at our heads, feeling the bass beat through the carpet at our backs. I had the biggest crush on Bobby all through high school, but he was popular and always had a girlfriend, which was never me. To be fair, I never told him how I felt because I didn't want to chance ruining our friendship. I enjoyed his company and settled on being his friend.

"Don't you guys go making whoopee, now!" Bobby's great-grandma would say to us before we left the house on a Saturday night. We would laugh, embarrassingly, because we never knew if she meant to party or have sex.

Every weekend we hung out at someone's house; whoever's parents were gone. Occasionally, this meant my house because my parents had bought a cabin when I started high school and they would go there often to get away for the weekend. My group of friends was respectful and caring, even with a case of cheap beer in them. They always made sure to help clean up, leaving no evidence a party had occurred.

These high school boys were the boys that loved me as their friend, but also taught me how guys think and behave, and I loved them dearly. If only I'd recognized then that they were trying to save me from the guy who was nothing like them, the guy I would end up marrying, and later, despising.

As a senior in high school, I was to choose the path the rest of my life would take, and I had two top contenders that had absolutely nothing to do with each other; I needed help deciding. I have always been fascinated by pregnancy, labor and delivery, and newborns, and I've also always had an interest in fashion.

My family would often say things like "You'd make a garbage bag look fashionable!" This would make me laugh because I could imagine people walking the runway in black and white garbage bags as outfits. I just really loved reading fashion magazines and had only ever had jobs in clothing stores. My first job at 15 was as a fragrance gift-set wrapper at Bloomingdale's before the Christmas season, and from there on I was hooked on retail. Throughout high school, I worked in a women's clothing store at the Mall of America, which had opened just as I became a teenager. People loved the mall in the 90s, and I felt important working there. I wasn't comfortable in sales, but I loved setting displays and restocking the inventory.

College can be really intimidating because it's where a person is supposed to declare what it is that they want to do for the rest of their life, but what if we're just not sure? We can't test things out for a while and see what we'd like; the four-year plan is laid out based on whatever a person declares for their major, so students have to decide early what type of job they'll want to have.

Dad had done rounds at the local hospital, so he knew people in labor and delivery. He was able to set me up with an "informational interview," where I got to assist in a couple of births to see what it was all about. I had never even been in a hospital before that first day; I was nervous, excited, and scared, but I loved it all.

I put my scrubs on and went to sit in the nurse's station, watching the rows of monitors light up with the glowing peaks and valleys of contractions in each of the various labor and delivery rooms. The nurse that I was shadowing was very gentle, kind, and caring, and she taught me how to tell what a contraction looked like on the screen, and when we needed to go check the patients. She could've been annoyed that I knew nothing about anything in that room, that I was something extra added to her already busy day, but she wasn't. She loved what she did, and she was excited to share her experience with a newbie. She made me feel comfortable in a space where I was not only ignorant but completely naïve as to what birth looks like.

I vividly remember two births during my two-day stint as a wannabe L&D nurse. Having never been pregnant, nor witnessed any births before, it was an exhilarating and also haunting experience. It was suddenly "go" time and we went into the delivery room where I was met with another woman's vagina, legs spread wide open, monitors loudly signaling the massive waves of contractions; the smell of sweat, amniotic fluid and disinfectant mixing in the air.

Suddenly I felt scared; what the hell was I supposed to be doing? The *actual* nurse asked me to hold the patient's leg so she can start pushing. Ummm, what? I thought I was just a spectator here! But I quickly grabbed her leg, which felt much heavier than I imagined a leg should be. She'd had an epidural and could not help in supporting the weight of her bottom half, so our job was to help her navigate this impending delivery.

I had finally adjusted to my surroundings and gotten into the groove of the leg holding and hearing the "PUSH" to the count of ten when something went suddenly wrong. The nurse was pushing the big red button on the wall, yelling some color-coded

"CODE" and people were scrambling all around the room. The nurse yelled to me to go tell the other nurses back at the nurse's station the same code color, and I had no idea what was happening.

More people came into the room and I found myself standing in the back of the room watching the experts do exactly what they are trained to do, almost instinctively. To be honest, I don't really remember what happened from there. I think I was partially traumatized by the whole experience, and my mind failed to imprint the remaining events of the delivery. Part of me thinks I ended up back at the nurse's station leaving the real nurses to do their thing, and part of me thinks they ended up moving her to an emergency C-section. Either way, I don't remember watching the baby be born that day, but I know it happened, and I know that everything ended up ok.

The other birth that stands out to me is one that rocked my suburban-white-girl world. This patient was from an African country and did not speak English. She did not have a birth partner or anyone in the room with her. When we walked into that room, she looked at me with fear in her eyes and needed someone to tell her it would be ok. Not being able to communicate through language, I held her hand until it was time to hold her leg to push.

We had her do a few pushes, but it wasn't quite time, so the nurse and I went back out to the nurse's station to watch the monitors for a bit. I felt sad for this woman and guilty for leaving her to labor alone. But there are several patients needing attention and only so many nurses to go around.

The nurse asked me if I noticed anything unusual about the previous patient's vagina. Did she remember that I was new around here? Everything about another woman's vagina was unusual to me, much less a laboring woman's vagina! She then told me that the woman had been a victim of genital mutilation and there was nothing left but a small hole. She would need to be cut for a second time so the baby could pass through.

Once again, we were back in the delivery room with the woman and this time, she was ready. The doctor came in to do his thing, and the nurse and I were on either side of him, each holding a leg while she pushed. I lost track of time and reality and before I knew it, the baby was out, and they'd whisked it across the room to examine.

I stood there, somewhat in shock of what just happened, overcome with emotion, and fighting back hot tears at the beautiful cries coming from the corner behind me. I was just a part of this incredible experience and was in awe of what went into delivering a baby into the world. But the other nurses were just doing their jobs and were not as overcome by the beauty of the moment as I was. For them, this was just a day in the life of a labor and delivery nurse.

It was time for me to leave for the day, which also happened to be the last time I'd step foot in a hospital until my own babies were born years later. I went into the locker room and changed out of my scrubs, leaving them in the hamper as some sort of last goodbye to the path I did not choose to take. As an eighteen-year-old girl who had never even been in a hospital before, witnessing the miracle and messiness of birth convinced me I was not ready to choose nursing as my career.

It had been instilled in me that I would go to the University of Minnesota because that's where both of my parents graduated from. But I didn't think I was ready for the giant vastness of the Twin Cities college campus, so I decided to go to the smaller Duluth campus. Duluth is a charming port city on Lake Superior, located in northeastern Minnesota. There are tunnels between campus buildings because it's often too cold to venture outside, even just to get from class to class. I've always disliked the cold and thought I belonged in California. In fact, the only two colleges I applied to were the University in Duluth and San Diego

State University. But, instead of taking study breaks on the warm, sunny beaches of California, I was stuck in a city where everyone wore flannel, drank beer, and enjoyed outdoor winter activities in the snow. Somehow, the universe kept me close to home and allowed me to meet a man that would slowly knock me down and break me to my core.

And So It Begins

I had just turned 19 when I met Scott. I was at an age when I had very few life experiences, yet went after everything with abandon, the age when despite all that I did not yet know, I thought I knew everything. It was 1999, and I had come back home from my first semester at college to be with family and friends over Thanksgiving break. Saturday night, my girlfriends and I went out to a dance club downtown, which was something we'd done together since we were sixteen. The late 1990s and early 2000s were a time of Britney Spears and boy bands; a time to wear short skirts or pleather pants and belly-showing tank tops, which we proudly donned.

Our night out began as usual, getting glammed up to head to the club. We'd had a few years of experience navigating the dance floor and dodging unwanted advances from boys with boners, but this time, I learned my girls had befriended some of those boys while I was away at school. We'd been at the club for at least an hour when my girlfriends began acting very familiar and friendly with a group of guys. This wasn't something we normally *did* at the club, and I felt like I was excluded from some secret, like an outsider among my best friends. There were three of us girls and five guys; the playing field wasn't level.

I thought these must be some special guys if my girls had gotten to know them well enough to meet up. They were laughing together, sharing inside jokes, and seemed to like hanging out, but I was annoyed they hadn't warned me of this new friendship before we got there and that these guys would now be included in our night out. I got over my bitterness quickly, and we all became fast friends.

One of those boys was Scott. He had a girlfriend at the time, although she was never with him when we hung out. Scott seemed aloof, almost acting as if he were above the rest of us. He was a couple of years older than most of the group, and he played the role of the annoyed older brother well. Even still, we continued to hang out, especially once my girl Heidi and his buddy Nate started dating. The group became inseparable, and I drove the two and a half hours home from college every weekend so that we could hang out.

On top of missing my friends at home, I was on the verge of being kicked out of college. There was a three-strike rule in the dorms; I'd been written up twice within the first three months of school and was borderline rebellious in my RA's eyes. Some people had cool Resident Assistants, but mine was determined to be a fun *ruiner*.

The first time I got in trouble I was sitting in my neighbor's dorm room, in the middle of the afternoon, watching T.V. The three of us were in our sweats, just hanging out with the door open for anyone to pop in for a visit. The RA walked in and noticed that there were bottles of alcohol sitting up on the shelf. They were filled with water and highlighter ink, which was a cool thing to do in the late 90s - use black lights and highlighters to make things glow. It was obvious we had not recently consumed the alcohol from those bottles, and they weren't even in my room, yet bitchy McFee wrote us all up anyway.

The second time I had "seriously misbehaved" was when I was visiting some friends in the afternoon on another floor of my dorm. Their door was wide open, and I was standing in the doorway chatting when along came their RA to check up on the group. I moved out of the doorway into the hall, and he peeked into the room, saying, "Oh, what's that on the floor there under your bed?" It was a bottle of alcohol and another ticket for me. At this point, I was afraid to go anywhere outside of my own room because just one more of those "incidents" would be my demise. I decided to save them the trouble, and call it quits on my own. I moved home.

Our new group was hanging out regularly, now. We'd go dancing or out to dinner, but mostly we just hung out at the guys' houses because they were older than us and we could have some drinks at their place. Scott had broken up with his girlfriend at some point and, not one to stay single for long, made it his mission to pursue me. I didn't find him attractive, and I didn't like his personality. He was arrogant and the only conversations he had were surface-level, filled with humor and jokes. While I didn't feel any emotional or physical connection to him, I loved the attention he gave me; *that* was exciting and new. I was a nineteen-year-old girl who hadn't had any serious boyfriends before, and the guys in my life had always been just close friends. Years later, this would become a point of contention between Scott and me; he'd make fun of me for never having a serious boyfriend before him, telling me how "crazy" that was given that he'd been dating and having sex since he was fifteen. It was the idea of being uninvolved that was crazy to him, "Why *wouldn't* you have boyfriends? There must be something wrong with you if you've never had a boyfriend…"

I had massive crushes on a few guys in high school, like with Bobby, but I didn't know what to do with those feelings so I just kept diaries and wrote love letters that stayed sealed in a box in my closet. If only I had dared to let my heart speak I would have probably found some pretty great romances. Instead, I listened to my inner voice telling me I wasn't good enough, and that if I were, a boy would have asked me out by now.

I purposely lost my virginity to Jake, one of my guy friends, the summer before college just so my first experience wouldn't be with a random guy in college. In hindsight, it was a terrible decision, but I had never really held my virginity sacred and so went into it thinking, *why not*. Jake was in the grade above me and was home for the summer. We had flirted over the years, getting handsy when we'd had too much to drink. No one took Jake seriously as he was a partier and a womanizer, but he was fun to be around at parties and a great kisser. I don't remember informing him of my decision to have sex with him beforehand, but I asked him to come over to my house late one night to hang out. He obliged and we ended up having sex on the couch in my parent's basement while everyone else was asleep. It wasn't good, but he was gentle and made sure I was comfortable the entire time. When we were done, I thought that I would feel different, but the only difference was that I could say I wasn't a virgin. I think I trusted myself with him because I knew he was experienced with sex and would be able to show me how it was done.

The first night Scott kissed me, our group was at a bar playing darts. The guys were drinking, and because we were still underage, we were not. Throughout the night, Scott kept flirting with me and grabbing my butt whenever I'd come back to the table after my turn throwing darts. I was getting thoroughly annoyed, eventually giving up playing darts just so that I could stay seated. It had turned into a joke with him because he could tell it was annoying me, so he continued, laughing it off every time.

Towards the end of the night, the group made the decision that I should drive Scott home since I was sober, and he was not. It was also a ploy to try to hook us up; they'd been witnesses to his flirting attempts all night and must've thought we'd hit it off. He drove a brand-new, silver F-150 Ford truck. It was a demo vehicle from the dealership where he worked, and I hadn't ever driven a truck before. I felt tiny behind the wheel, a million miles away from him in the passenger seat. On the way to his house, he droned on about how drunk he was and how "lame" I was for not being drunk too.

We obviously weren't in a position to have any real conversation of substance, but I was naïve and quickly became accustomed to this type of small talk. I'd spent the entire night annoyed with his behavior, how could this moment in time become the start of a relationship leading to marriage and kids? This was the first guy to show me any outright affection and I guess I enjoyed it.

I pulled into his driveway, and before we got out of the truck, he leaned over, closing the million-mile gap between us, and kissed me. I kissed back. It wasn't even a good kiss, but it came with the element of surprise and was heavy with his desire, so I let it continue. Thus, began our relationship; a drunken, one-sided, sloppy kiss was the beginning of years of manipulation.

I don't know how our relationship officially started. After the kiss goodnight, I got in my car and drove home, not giving "what happens now?" much thought. When our group was together, we were together, and over time we morphed into a couple. Scott wasn't like my friends from high school; he was an adult with a full-time job, his own house, and seemed to have life pretty figured out. He was mature in an "I'll take care of you" way, which felt grown-up and appealed to me now that I was on my own. Scott opened doors and paid the bill, but he was not a romantic; he knew these were things guys were *supposed* to do to impress a girl. I put my blinders on and just enjoyed the ride. He joked, but we joked together. We had inside jokes, laughed often, and had fun in everything we did together.

Since I had moved home from college and took a semester off

from school, I needed to get a job. Shortly after we started dating, Scott got me a job working as a cashier at the car dealership where he sold cars. Oh, how working there, with all of those bored men, gave me some thick skin! They'd prank-call the cashier line, pretending to be a creepy customer, whispering into the phone "what color panties are you wearing?" And every time, I'd sit there, jaw wide open from the shock of what just happened. They'd comment on my clothes, "Mmmm, I *really* like this belt." while grabbing the end of it, forcing me to respond in an uncomfortable "Thanks" while backing away. It still gives me the creeps thinking about it.

On our four-month anniversary, Scott brought me four white roses. I didn't even know it was something worth celebrating. Standing behind the service garage's cashier counter at work, I greeted him cheerfully when I saw him walk up. "Hey! When did you get here?"

He looked at me, sort of gave a quick smile and said, "Here" while handing me the roses, then turned and walked away. Once the immediate "What just happened?" shock wore off, I looked down at the flowers and pulled out the little card that read, "Happy four months!"

I smiled to myself as there was no one else around. Then I had a slew of emotions all at once. "That was weird!" I thought. Why hadn't he said anything? Was he embarrassed? Now I'm embarrassed because no one is around and I'm standing here all alone holding flowers that I'll certainly need to explain to everyone that comes to the cashier counter. While it was cute and endearing, I think the real reason he brought them was so that everyone would know we were together. Within minutes, some of the sales guys came up to the counter to see the flowers and "congratulate" me. It felt forced and a little awkward, but I just thought it was me that was awkward.

We had only worked together for a couple of months when Scott left to go to another car dealership, while I stayed on full-time at the original dealership for another three years while taking college courses at night. I was promoted quickly to the business office, and it felt nice to be moving up and proving myself without him around. I had gotten the job because of him, and I often felt that our coworkers thought less of me because of that. I learned that people didn't like him, and I think that opinion rubbed off onto them not liking me by association until they got to know me without him around.

After work one Friday night, a few of the girls from the office invited me out for a drink. I was newly twenty-one and was excited to be able to hang out with them away from work. A couple of hours and appetizers later, I started to feel the effect of the beers I'd had much more than I thought I should. I had stuck with beer because I knew that I could have a couple and still be ok to drive later, especially over a few hours and having some food. But that wasn't the case; I started to feel extremely drowsy and nauseous. Knowing I wouldn't be able to drive home, I called Scott and asked him to pick me up. He was annoyed that I'd allowed myself to get too drunk to drive, but I convinced him that something was off, and I needed his help.

Twenty minutes later, Scott arrived, and I said my goodbyes, trying to keep myself together while meeting him in the entryway of the bar. He escorted me to his truck and once inside, I immediately laid my head down on the open window frame of the passenger seat's door. Not ten seconds after Scott started to drive, my head was out the window and my stomach's contents were spewed outside and along the side of the truck from the wind.

"How in the hell did you get so drunk? You couldn't go out for just a couple beers and not get smashed?" Scott demanded.

He kept berating me, making me feel childish and stupid for even going out at all. He brought me back to his apartment where I crawled into the bathroom to continue my vomiting. I couldn't see straight, only able to lift my head from the floor long enough to lay it on the toilet seat again.

"I'm going back to the bar," Scott came in to tell me, "I saw an old girlfriend there and I want to go back and hang out with her."

Confused, I couldn't tell if what he was saying was true. Was he going to leave me like this? Did he really see her there, or did he make something up because he's trying to get back at me for getting drunk? I was too lethargic to even respond. Moments after he left the bathroom, his roommate, Joe, came in and brought me a pillow, blanket, and a glass of water. Joe took care of me while my boyfriend told me he was ashamed of me and left to go meet up with an old girlfriend, or so he said.

I've thought a lot about this moment over the years. I wasn't one to drink too much, and I rarely drank unless I was with Scott, so he knew my typical behavior. It was not typical for me to have such a reaction to drinking two or three beers, and the only plausible solution I have come up with is that I must've been roofied at the bar. I don't know where Scott went that night. I asked him several times and always got the same response – the same one he'd originally given. I didn't believe him, and I thought it was just an excuse as a way to get back at me. But for fear of being continually tormented about my own behavior that night, I didn't push for an answer.

Since I had just started college when I met Scott, I still got together frequently with my high school friends. They would tell me they didn't like Scott, and he would tell me he didn't like that I was hanging out with other guys, so I slowly stopped seeing them. It wasn't obvious to me then, but my world got much smaller once I started eliminating the people and things Scott didn't like.

We seldom stayed at my house, but of course, the one rare time we did, one of those old guy friends called me (*on the house phone, no less*). It was around midnight and we were just falling asleep when the phone in my bedroom started to ring. I never got

29

phone calls, especially not in the middle of the night, so I was surprised. I felt along the floor under my bed, feeling around for the transparent aqua-blue phone, tossing aside the "boob cream" along the way.

"Do you *really* think that cream will do anything to help your tiny tits?" Scott asked when I told him I'd ordered the cream. All you had to do was massage the cream on your breasts twice a day and it was supposed to help give them volume. I was so self-conscious of my B-cups that I was willing to give anything a try. It didn't work, of course.

"Why don't you just get implants?" Scott asked, mostly suggesting.

"I plan to! But not until I'm done having kids, so I have a while."

I finally found the phone after several rings. There wasn't caller-ID so I couldn't screen the call, but I answered it anyway.

"Hello?" I asked, in a somewhat irritated tone. Who would be calling at midnight?

"What's up, Jess?" I knew right away it was Bobby, who also happened to be the cousin of my best friend and roommate at the time. We chatted for a few minutes and I could feel Scott's tension and irritation growing beside me in the bed.

I started to get nervous and sweaty but tried to sound light-hearted "I have to get going, but I'll let Brooke know you called!"

Bobby gave a questioning laugh and said, "Ok then." I knew he had called for me, but I was trying to smooth things over with Scott before hanging up. After I hung up, I found myself apologizing and making excuses for why he might have called. Scott said nothing and just rolled away from me and would not talk to me, falling asleep giving me the silent treatment.

He would often bring that event up to punish me later, claiming that I must be cheating on him, because why else would "random guys" be calling me in the middle of the night. I tried to defend the situation and begged Scott to remember that Bobby was just a good friend from high school, but it didn't matter; I was in trouble. So, to avoid making him upset and causing fights, I stopped contacting my high school friends and made excuses for why I was never free to hang out.

I missed those friends a lot and hated that I couldn't talk with them or see them without getting into trouble with Scott. But it also felt nice to have someone care about me enough to want me all to himself, and I didn't want to make him jealous unnecessarily. In retrospect, I see how strange it was that I had to prove to him that I loved only him by eliminating any friends or family who may have tried to save me from him. But back then, only his opinion and his approval mattered.

By now, the friends I'd had when Scott and I met were no longer my close friends. They had begun their own relationships, and we rarely had time to get together. I learned later that they just didn't like Scott and were perfectly ok not hanging out with him—and by extension me—that often. I didn't have many other friends at that time, but I hardly noticed because I loved spending my free time with Scott. I worked, went to school, and hung out with him. He was still arrogant but played house well; he was the grown-up in our relationship, guiding me in life's purpose and experiences. Scott had lofty goals and seemed to have it all together; a successful job, a healthy social life, and was genuinely fun to be around. He pushed me to also have goals and we enjoyed planning our future together.

Scott played in several softball leagues, so our summer nights and weekends were usually around the field for games and tournaments. I was his supportive cheerleader, and his teammates became our friends. He was generous with his time and friendship; he'd play whenever people needed someone to fill in, always there to help out.

A couple of the teams he played on were co-ed, yet he never asked me to play. I'd played softball for years in school but I never asked to play with him; those guys and girls were competitive and

I'm not. Their intensity and attitudes towards the game would've just made me uncomfortable, and Scott wanted me just where I was: on the sidelines, cheering him on. He didn't want to take any chance of it being the other way around.

I know now that the reason he volunteered to play for any team that was down a player was that he desired to be *"needed."* He was the pitcher, front and center, always. He loved attention, and I loved to make other people happy, so I would do what I could to give him the attention, praise, and adoration he desired. I showed up to every softball game, even though I sat alone nearly every time, just because I knew he wanted me there. I went to his house and shampooed the carpets while he was at work, just because it was something he had wanted to get done for a long time, and I had the time to do it. He came home from work to find me waiting, beaming with pride at my accomplishment. He smiled and said, weakly, "Thank you," but his reactions to my efforts were so diluted that I felt like I would just have to try even harder the next time.

When your boyfriend is also your best friend, you want to make sure he's happy. He'd suggest I'd dress a certain way, make my hair blonder, or work harder at my job to move up faster. I took his suggestions to heart, internalizing them as a path to make him happy, and to give him reasons to feel proud of me. In return, he'd tell me I looked sexy, or that he was proud of my accomplishments. That little bit of praise was all I needed to keep trying to please him. The thing I learned too late was that looking sexy is not the same as looking beautiful, and being proud translated to, "I get to show you off," which is not the same as "I love you for who you are."

When I turned the *legal* drinking age of 21 (yes, I had my fair share of drinking illegally, but never once got caught!), my parents were just beginning their journey into divorce. My dad had been having an affair, but none of us knew yet.

One Friday night, there was a fire in the apartment complex

next to mine and the building was evacuated. I had just gotten into bed when the smoke alarms started blaring in the hallway. Opening the front door slightly, I peeked out into the hallway to see two firemen telling everyone to get outside. This was not a drill. I threw my robe on over my pajamas, grabbed my purse and shoes, and headed out the door. It was one of those moments where I knew everything would be alright but was terrified just the same.

It was late fall and cold outside, so I was not about to stand outside until they gave us the all-clear to head back in. I grabbed some clothes, bundled up, and got in my car, driving to stay at my parent's house for the night. It was probably midnight by the time I got there and settled into my temporary bed on the floor in front of the fireplace in the living room. Mom was there with me, chatting to calm my nerves about potentially not having an apartment to go back to in the morning.

In walked Dad from a night out with some buddies, dressed far too well for such a casual get-together. He was pleasantly surprised to see me and stayed to hear the story of why I was spending the night on their living room floor. After ten minutes or so, he said "Well, I'm running for president in the morning, so I better get some sleep." I replied with an "Ok" as in, "If you say so!" with almost a snicker as I assumed he had just had too much to drink and was making up stories. Once he was out of earshot, I asked Mom, "What was that all about? Why did he say he's running for President?"

I imagined he had put his name into the hat to run for the POTUS, which made me laugh because our family members are not politicians. Turned out he was running for President of the Board at his clinic. I don't remember the outcome of that election, but I do remember that my apartment didn't burn down, and I was able to return in the morning. I also remember that this was one of the last times I spent with my parents while still "happily" married. They weren't happy, but none of us knew any differently because they behaved as they always had – cordial and friendly toward each other.

Dad wasn't out with buddies that night, he had been out with another woman. I don't know if Mom knew it then, but she never let on if she did. We simply never talked about it. I wasn't living at home then and didn't talk to either of my parents with any frequency. I think Mom must've known something was going on but didn't confront him about it. When she finally did officially find out, she was angry. She sobbed and yelled and told him to get out, which he did. He went to stay with his mistress while her husband was living in their basement, dying of cancer. They found themselves in a position where they were in lust but with nowhere to go.

My youngest sisters were not yet in junior high and they were the ones still at home with a front-row seat to the demise of our parent's relationship. Dad would tell Mom he still loved her and she would tell him she knew he was just having a midlife crisis. Mom tried to make it work for far too long, telling Dad, "The grass isn't going to be greener on the other side. This isn't really what you want."

He would go back to living with Mom for a while, and then back with his mistress, a cycle that went on for months. One of my sisters would call me to say, "It happened again," meaning Mom had caught Dad in another lie. I wanted to make things better for my sisters, but also wanted nothing to do with my parent's personal life. I didn't know how to do one without the other, so I tried to stay out of it completely.

Mom was Dad's first love and she took his virginity. We all presumed Dad was having a midlife crisis, and Mom was willing to give him the time to sort himself out. After what felt like years of back and forth, they officially divorced. It seems common to hear that couples wait until their children are out of the house before they decide to get divorced, and I just don't understand the point of that! Now the children know that your whole relationship was a lie and that their parents were miserable for years. What does that teach the kids? I will say, as a child whose parents divorced just as I was learning how to be in my own adult relationship, it messes with your perspective of what a marriage should be. Up until Scott and I started to get serious in our relationship, no one in my family had been divorced and I had no idea what it felt like. Surprisingly, about three years into our relationship several of my family members went through a divorce, and it made me question everything I thought love and marriage were. In hindsight, that probably made me more vulnerable to Scott's suave and attention.

I cried to Scott one night, "Who would want me now? I come with baggage!"

He responded while wrapping me in a hug, "That won't be us; we will never be like them. My parents are still married and we'll follow their path."

I trusted him and wanted to believe that he could predict our future. I didn't go out with girlfriends and talk about relationships, instead, I worked full-time during the day and went to college classes at night. When I wasn't working or at school, I was with Scott. My parents were going through their divorce and I stopped looking to them for guidance. There was no one to hear the details of my life; I talked about everything with Scott, and it strengthened our bond, making us feel close, special, and devoted.

I was spending more and more time at his house, working on home improvement tasks together, making dinners on weeknights, and generally playing house. We traveled a lot, places like Vegas or Mexico, staying at fancy hotels and acting much older than we were. Scott made good money for someone our age and he liked to spend it, buying me Juicy Couture tracksuits (they were the "in" thing then!), handing me a couple of hundred-dollar bills to play the slot machines at the casino, or sending me on trips to a day spa to be pampered. I didn't feel worthy of these things, I was only a broke college student, but I knew it made him happy to prove he could do them, so I accepted the gifts.

When I bought my first car, it had a manual stick-shift, which I had no idea how to drive. Scott was there with me when I signed the paperwork, and he drove it home, committing to teach me how to drive it later. He took me to parking lots, patiently instructing me to ease up on the clutch while simultaneously pressing the gas pedal. He didn't get upset when we'd jerk back and forth or if I'd kill the engine because I just couldn't get it right. He was my boyfriend but also a lot like a father figure to me.

We didn't talk much about my parent's divorce, Scott and I. He gave me an escape from the situation, and I think we were both comfortable avoiding my parents altogether. Scott was intimidated by them, as he was with most people that didn't cater to him. My parents were cordial with Scott, but I knew they didn't respect him very much because he was so cocky and arrogant.

We spent a lot of time with Scott's parents, inviting them to join us at the reserved chef's table at a high-end restaurant, the seats on the fifty-yard-line at the Viking's game, or the expensive trendy steakhouse downtown because they were the only people we knew well that could afford to enjoy these experiences with us. We appreciated their company and looked up to them in their still-standing relationship.

The Drug Friend

S cott and I had been dating for at least three years and I spent almost all my time at his place, only going to mine when I needed more clothes or if he was going out with the guys. I was still in college and living in a condo on the opposite side of town, but my job was close to his house, so I often stayed with him out of convenience. Plus, we also really enjoyed spending time together. He lived with his cousin, who also happened to be one of his closest friends, and we all got along great! We'd often hang out together on nights and weekends, going out for dinner or watching movies in the living room, roommates but also friends.

One particular Saturday night, Scott went out with his friends and I went to his house after work to wait for him, planning to spend the night as I typically did on the weekends. I knew he was going out, but it wasn't unusual for me to hang out at his house alone. We didn't work the same schedule and he liked knowing that I was at home waiting for him. We were nearly living together by then, and I spent more time there than at my place.

I texted him when I left work to let him know I was going to his house to stay the night.

"Just leaving work. I'm going to stay at your house tonight, so I'll see you when you get home. Have fun!"

I didn't get a response, which was unusual, but not that odd given that he was probably at the bar where it was loud, or it was just assumed I would be there when he got home. Scott and his cousin lived in an end-unit townhouse, and I parked along the street next to the driveway so that I wasn't blocking the driveway or garage when they got home.

I watched TV for a while before going upstairs to get ready for bed. In my pajamas, I had just finished brushing my teeth when I heard them come home. I waited in bed for a few minutes, expecting that Scott would pop up to greet me, but when he didn't come up to say hello, I texted him to tell him I was upstairs. I was in my PJs in bed and didn't want to saunter down into the bright lights of the kitchen. Again, no response. This man had his phone glued to him 100% of the time, so the fact that he wasn't responding surely meant that he had lost his phone or was other-wise preoccupied.

After probably 15 minutes of hearing what sounded like a party had arrived at the house, and still no word from Scott, I went to the top of the stairs to listen closer. There was music playing and people talking and laughing, but I couldn't quite make out who it was, or even how many people there were. I was getting more and more irritated that he hadn't come up to see me, nor responded to any of my texts. *Was he mad at me? Did he not want me here? Why was I not invited to this party?* I went back into his room to put some decent clothes on and went back to the top of the stairs where I decided I just needed to go make my presence known.

I hopped down the carpeted stairs, making sure that my steps were loud enough to be heard coming. I was just over halfway down the stairs when a girl came into view, standing with her back against the counter, angled so that I could see just the side of her, engaged in conversation with someone in the kitchen. My stomach dropped a bit because I didn't know who she was, and it appeared that it was only her and Scott in the house.

She saw me right away, but as I took another couple steps down he came into view, shocked to be seeing me. He immediately said, "Hey, what are you doing here?" somewhat lightheartedly as to not seem so caught off guard, and somewhat terrified as hell to be seeing me.

I replied in an equally lighthearted tone as to not seem as irritated about the situation as I was, "I texted you a few times to let you know I was here. And my car is sitting right outside!"

Was he *really* trying to play dumb? He clearly hadn't seen any of my messages or he wouldn't be standing in "our" kitchen with another girl. But how had he not checked his phone in hours?

She was drunk and looked horrified to be seeing me. He quickly tried to recover, saying, "This is Angela," thinking that introducing me to this woman standing in our kitchen would reduce the tension that was filling the room.

Relief poured over me and I started to say "Oh, yea! Angie the drug friend!" but he cut me off before I could get it all out because she had no idea that's what they (we) called her. Her name was Angela, or Angie, depending on who was doing the introduction, and she was a friend that Scott and his cousin knew from somewhere, probably the old dance club days. They called her "the drug friend" because she always had ecstasy or something with her, while the rest of our group did not partake.

But my relief was short-lived; apparently, he hadn't seen my car nor any of the texts I had sent him. She must've been incredibly captivating! They were both drunk and it was obvious that I had interrupted something.

"Hi, I'm Jessica!" I said, finishing my descent down the stairs. She looked at him and in her drunken state immediately started sobbing, knowing that I was meant to be there, and she was not.

She looked at me and cried, "I thought you guys broke up!"

He immediately rushed to her, trying to comfort her while

ushering her to the front door. Wailing, she went outside and called a friend to come and pick her up. I sat down at the bottom of the stairs where I had been standing moments ago, just taking it all in. He kept going out to check on her and then come back in to check on me, seemingly enjoying having two girls upset with him. I don't know that I could place it at the time, his pleasure in the drama, but there was certainly no remorse or sense of being the source of the discomfort for the two women in his house.

"Typical drug friend," Scott said to me with an eye-roll, "she's so dramatic, always crying about something."

I didn't know how to respond, mostly just nodding at his remarks, waiting for her to be gone to actually talk about what was happening.

"Nothing happened," he said, "we were just out at the bar and she was too drunk to drive home, so I brought her here."

"She didn't have any friends with her?" I asked, skeptical. He made up some excuse about her meeting them after work and blah blah blah. Finally, her friend showed up and took her away, and we went up to bed as if nothing had happened at all. The lie about her being too drunk to drive was certainly believable, and he played the "I'm a nice guy" act well enough that I accepted it as a plausible situation.

I lie there next to him in bed, asking question after question, trying to get to the truth. But he wouldn't let me find the truth; every question was met with a brushed-off non-answer until I eventually gave up.

Then he turned it on me, "If you wouldn't have been playing Spiderman, sneaking around the house, this never would have happened."

I responded, "I WASN'T!! I texted you to let you know I was coming to stay the night, and then again to let you know I was upstairs once I heard you were home."

He kept antagonizing me, "And where's your car? Did you hide it down the road and cover it with leaves so I couldn't see it?"

I was irritated now, "My car is sitting right next to the driveway and it's not my fault you didn't see it." I was now having to defend my actions of being at my boyfriend's house, as if I were the one that did something wrong, rather than him getting caught with another girl. *Surely,* I should have sent a carrier pigeon with a note instead of simply texting that I would be at his house.

I found myself apologizing for even coming over and that next time I would make sure he knew ahead of time. It was me that was the one that had to make up to him for catching him with another girl because I didn't notify him well enough that I was going to be at his house.

We fell asleep together, just as we had for countless nights before, not processing what had just occurred only an hour before.

I should have left when she did. I should have driven off and never come back, but I stayed. I allowed him to tell me that she was a long-time friend (he had talked about her in the past) and that nothing happened or was going to happen. I only half-believed it, which is why I didn't leave; I just didn't know for sure. I wanted to believe him, and as someone that finds it nearly impossible to lie, it's hard to imagine someone you love can lie to you, over and over and over.

CEO

Once I finished my Associate's degree in liberal arts at the community college, I transferred to the school I originally thought was far too big for me, the University of Minnesota – Twin Cities campus. It was not the big, scary giant that I had unnecessarily feared and I found my way around pretty quickly. I quit my job at the car dealership and focused solely on school.

After eliminating nursing as a career path, I pursued a degree in Retail Merchandising. Interestingly, this degree was considered a Bachelor's in Science; I had no idea that retail was a scientific study! I felt incredibly fortunate to have chosen it as my field of study because the curriculum was business-based and granted me a lot of opportunities in my career. I have an entrepreneurial spirit and love the research and planning stages of things. I'm terrible at follow-through, but I can sure research the heck out of something!

I didn't live on campus; I rented a condo for a while and then a townhouse in the suburbs with my sister, Marie, driving into school every day. Parking was the hardest part about the whole thing, especially in the brutally freezing winters where half of the parking lots were filled with enormous piles of snow, making available spaces even harder to come by.

Since I didn't start my major with a cohort in my classes, I felt like an outsider, not really belonging and not sharing the same experience. I felt older because I had spent the previous three years working full-time, spending my nights at school while the rest of my classmates were living their best college life. Most people in my classes wanted to work for Target, Best Buy, or some other major retailer as a buyer. The ability to get paid to travel the world and SHOP for a living sounded like a dream come true! However, I just couldn't see myself working for a huge corporation, doing things *their* way. I wanted to do things my way and decided in my senior year of college that I wanted to open my *own* store. It kind of just jumped at me, like *this is what I am going to be doing* and it all fell into place from there. I had my love of all things baby as my north star and developed everything around that. Any and all papers or projects that year were submitted based on research used for my store.

Fortunately, my aunt, Sara, had recently opened a jewelry boutique and I was able to take my internship there. She didn't have a point-of-sale system (POS, which is a dual-acronym for this tool), and I decided that setting one up would be my internship project. I researched which system to buy, chose the proper model, and had it delivered to her shop.

I spent *weeks* working to get everything in the store a barcode and have it entered into the system. I walked around with the hand-held barcode scanner, printing out SKU tickets and price tags for every item in the store.

Every single day Sara would say, "I'm never going to get used to this, ya know."

And every time I would reply, "I don't care if you throw it all away once I'm done, I'm practicing!"

As odd as it may sound, I loved every minute of the research and planning stages of setting up shop. It was sort of like playing house or school as a kid. Sara never did get used to the barcode system and gave up on it shortly after I completed my internship with her.

I graduated in May 2005 with my degree in Retail and began preparing to open my very own boutique store almost immediately. I found the perfect location in a brand-new strip mall, just below one of the most sophisticated and popular salons in the area. I wrote a business plan, secured a small business loan (with Mom's help for the collateral) from the bank next door to where my store would be located. It was all coming to fruition!

The space I found to lease was brand new, so it had never been built out before, meaning I got to start from scratch. The accent wall behind the checkout counter was painted in bright yellow and white vertical stripes, the rest of the walls were the most perfect shade of hot pink, just slightly pinker than that of Pepto Bismol, and the ceiling was painted the perfect blue like the sky. It was very bright, cheerful, and fun.

To save money, I bought all of the fixtures at a used-fixtures-outlet. I turned family baby photos into black and white 8x10 framed pictures and hung them around the walls of the store and used my younger cousin's crib as a display for blankets and stuffed animals. I was ready to start filling the store with merchandise and couldn't have been more excited to begin.

The store opened in the fall of 2005, just months after I had graduated college. A typical buyer for a store, regardless of size, would attend markets and travel to large expos to research up-and-coming products. I didn't have the budget to be traveling, and I wanted to be open as soon as possible, so instead, I had spent the previous year searching online for all things "baby," choosing a few well-known brands, but preferring little-known and unique items. My focus was on all-natural and organic product lines, which hadn't yet gained the popularity they have now, and even though my customers loved this aspect, they weren't used to the price tag that came along with the purer, higher-quality goods.

I loved going into the store, proud of what I'd accomplished, my visions now in real life. I adored listening to everyone's stories for what brought them in or who they were shopping for, seeing all the sweet newborn babes in tow. The customer favorite was the teeny tiny newborn t-shirts that read "Brand New," hanging from the clothesline in the store windows. It was certainly a draw into the store! Once inside, they could browse while listening to Frank Sinatra and Dean Martin, the scent of baby powder filling the air from the clean-burning custom candles I sold.

Scott, however, wasn't thrilled that I wasn't having immediate success. Every day he'd ask me how sales were that day, almost always disappointed they weren't higher. He wanted me to branch out and get people to franchise new locations, doing nothing to help this venture other than to tell me it was something I needed to figure out how to do. He would tell people to get their "baby shit" from my store, but not know enough about what I carried to have any meaningful influence. Scott was mostly uninvolved throughout the entire process of getting the shop up and running. While he was proud of me for opening my store, telling everyone that I was the CEO of my own company, I think he was intimated that I was doing it all on my own. He knew I was intelligent and independent and that scared him a bit. Scott always joked about how he made it two weeks at the local community college before giving up. School just wasn't his thing, so he made it his goal to prove to the world that he could still be successful without a college degree.

Scott and I were living together now, and he had moved on from the car business to the financial industry instead. He worked for a large corporate bank, doing well for himself, and decided it was time to buy a real home rather than the townhouse we'd been living in. He didn't involve me in the process much, and I hadn't even really known he was looking. He'd mention it in passing, showing me houses he found online, but I didn't feel like he was actually asking my opinion or making me a part of the decision.

It was a snowy evening in December, about four months after my store opening, when we pulled up to the house in an executive golf course neighborhood. I was shocked that we'd be looking at such a big step up from the house we'd been living in, but he was excited to show me around and I was happy to be a participant on the tour. It was a sprawling rambler-style house, with the kitchen and living room to the left of the front entryway, the master bedroom and an office to the right. The downstairs opened up to a large living room and bar area with three bedrooms and a bonus room down the hall. It was massive for only the two of us.

Scott told me he wanted to put in an offer but had wanted to show me the house first to make sure I liked it, too. We both agreed that we loved the place, and before I knew it, we had a move-in date scheduled for early January. Other than the original tour, I wasn't included in the home buying experience. There were no cost analysis discussions or loan process conversations, but I wasn't necessarily surprised by that either; he frequently worked with mortgages, so he knew his way around a home loan, and I was self-employed with no income to speak of. Regardless, I was excited to be moving in together, officially. Even though the house was *technically* his since the loan was in his name only and we weren't married, he made me feel like it was *ours* and he was buying it for us. This was just the next step in our relationship and I was happy to be along for the ride.

Love is in the Air

Valentine's Day was the day we decided would be our anniversary. Scott and I started dating in early February, but we couldn't pinpoint the actual day that would have made it official, so we agreed on February 14th. On our sixth anniversary, I worked at my store all day but closed a little early so that we could celebrate Valentine's Day together. Scott wasn't thrilled that I spent so much time at the store; he felt business owners were supposed to have flexibility in their schedules and should be able to come and go when they wanted. I felt guilty closing early, but I figured customers would understand, given the holiday.

I walked into the house to see that Scott had an evening laid out for us. He told me he had a special dinner menu that he would be preparing in the kitchen while I was to enjoy an in-home massage in the living room, just off the kitchen.

It was nice to be so spoiled, but at the same time, it felt awkward to be lying face down on a massage table in my living room, trying to relax, while my boyfriend was banging around in the kitchen next to me. I was shocked that he planned to cook because that was typically *my* department, not his. *This must be a special occasion!*

The menu was lobster mac and cheese with roasted asparagus. I was fairly certain that he had bought everything either already prepared, or close to it because he was not someone with the culinary skills to make lobster mac and cheese at home. I kept trying not to laugh during the massage, thinking, "What is going on in there?"

He liked big gestures, and this was just another grand show, but even still, I was skeptical. This was a lot, even for him.

After my massage, I stood in my robe around the massage table with Scott and the masseuse, awkwardly making small talk as she packed everything up. She had become a part of our romantic Valentine's evening, but we had to wait for her to leave so we could continue.

"Ok then, thanks so much! Enjoy your evening." It was an awkward moment for me, waiting for another woman to leave my house so that I could enjoy a romantic dinner with my boyfriend.

As soon as she was out the door, Scott sent me on a scavenger hunt around the house. He handed me a slip of paper that read, "Where do we fall asleep at the end of the day?"

An obvious one to start.

From a pillow on our bed, I found another clue, "I like to take these with me on the golf course, but you hate the smell of them."

This brought me to his cigar box, for which the clue was correct – I hated the smell of cigars. The thick smoke lingering in the air, his breath smelling like hot garbage afterward. The hunt had me embarrassed because I didn't know what was going on or what to expect, and I don't like to be the center of attention; I felt like I was being watched, fumbling around, looking for clues. I didn't know if it was ok to be excited; I wanted to be because scavenger hunts are meant to be fun, but it was the unknown of it all that had me nervous. What would the end bring? Scott liked to joke around and I didn't want to get excited only to have him say "April Fools!" instead of "Happy Valentine's Day!"

The clues were typed on little strips of paper, and they

described things from our relationship that would lead me to the place where the next clue could be found. One of the last clues read, "We used to sleep in this bed when we were dating," which brought me to our guest bedroom, containing his old bedroom set.

The final clue was laying there, directing me to push play on the CD player in the corner of the room. But the song wouldn't start, so he ended up directing me from the closet in which he was hiding. Through a muffled voice within the closed doors, he said "You have to turn it back on first!"

I laughed, because the instructions had written, simply, "Press play on the stereo" and I didn't realize it wasn't actually on.

Finally, it started to play, and again, the voice within the closet muttered, "You'll have to come open the closet door." I did as he asked and found him down on one knee with a ring. He was just kneeling there, smiling.

"Oh, yea! Will you marry me?" he finally asked.

I was giddy, yet embarrassed, and full of excitement.

To end the suspense, I said "Yes!" and he got up on both feet where we hugged for a minute, before moving back upstairs to enjoy the meal he had prepared. We sat there, at the dining room table, both staring at the ring now on my finger. It was a simple, thin white-gold band with a solitaire diamond, the prongs stood up tall making it look larger than it was. He made sure to tell me that it was "A carat and a third," and that he "can't believe how expensive diamonds are!" Yet again, I felt embarrassed, knowing that it didn't have to be expensive or big for me to have said yes.

The proposal came as a complete surprise to me. It likely shouldn't have, we had just moved into *our* house, and I guess this was just the next logical step. When we first met I couldn't stand him; he was nothing like me nor any of my friends, but he showed me affection and helped me navigate through a very vulnerable time into adulthood. After a couple of years, I guess I just knew that someday we'd get married. We both did. We talked about our future goals and hopes and dreams as if they were ours together. I wasn't the type of girl to drop hints or ask when we'd get engaged, I just knew it would happen someday, not realizing that the someday was sooner than I expected. I was twenty-five, had my own business and we'd been in a long-term relationship already, it all seemed to be the right path to take. Looking back, perhaps my lack of enthusiasm about getting married meant I wasn't ready to get married yet, that I should have seen he wasn't *the one.* But I was comfortable and didn't know any better. This was still the only relationship I'd known, and with the demise of my parent's marriage, I didn't have much to compare it to either.

In the beginning, we shared a lot of the same goals and ambitions. We wanted the house in the suburbs, to travel, and someday, add children to our family. Although we didn't concretely discuss what our future would look like, we both felt that we were natural together and that eventually we would get married. I was the caregiver and made it perfectly clear that one day I wanted kids and to be a stay-at-home mom. He was comfortable with this because I was the one that wanted kids and he knew he was the breadwinner.

"You work for fun, anyway. You'll just have to hire people to run the store once we start having kids."

Working at the store that I created was indeed fun; it was my passion and I was incredibly proud of myself for the accomplishment. But as a young entrepreneur just starting out, there was no way I could have just "hired out" the work, either financially or logically. That was *my* baby! I would tell him as much, but he would just wave me off, and I figured we'd just address the issue when or if it came to fruition.

Scott was more of a financial caregiver; he liked nice things and enjoyed providing me with nice things. In his eyes, if he could buy me a big house and expensive cars, take our friends out to fancy dinners, and travel often, it meant he was successful.

The problem with wanting nice (expensive) things and

equating success to *having* nice things is that it's never enough. He always wanted more, and the desire for more became an addiction; getting to *more* took precedence over anything else, and he lost all moral ground to achieve this sense of *more*.

I have a lot of mixed feelings when I think back on that day we got engaged. While it was an exciting time for my naive, mid-twenties self, what I know now is that the early years of our relationship were not at all what a good relationship should've been. Even though I knew it at the time, deep down in the corner of my mind where things sit to fester, I blocked out the voice inside me saying *this is all wrong, this is not what it's supposed to be like.*

Everything in our relationship was about *him*, his wants and needs. He wanted us to appear a certain way, so the house he bought for us wasn't really for us at all; it was for him to show others that he was capable of buying such a house. I enjoyed being a caretaker – of him, of our new house, of all the things needing to be done to keep him happy, because it was just the two of us in this life together.

The next day I went back to work at my store, business as usual, except now I was engaged. We had called our parents the night before to let them know the news, and I remember being surprised at their reactions, or lack thereof. I expected Scott's mom to burst out sobbing with tears of joy because she was a happy crier, but instead, she gave a more muted "Oh, wow! Congratulations!"

I was fairly certain she wasn't privy to the impending engagement and seemed as surprised as I was. Mom gave a similar "Congrats!" because what else do you say when your daughter calls to tell you she's engaged?

Dad hadn't answered that night and called me back the following afternoon when I was at work. I answered the phone while sitting at the register.

"Hey, dad!"

"Hey, Jess. Sorry I didn't call you back sooner." We didn't chat

51

often, especially not on the phone, so it was a little unusual for both of us.

Quickly and cheerfully, I said, "I got engaged last night!"

I was giddy and full of excitement, expecting him to be excited for me as well. However, I was swiftly disappointed.

"Oh, yeah?" He started, before continuing, "Me too!"

My heart sank and my head seemed to start floating away, buzzing while trying to filter out the news from the other end of the line. He went on to tell me their engagement story, also taking place on Valentine's Day, and how excited *they* were. This was the woman he had, only a year or two before, been having an affair with while married to my mother. How could he possibly think I would be excited for him, and how could he not understand that that was not the time to convey such news? His oldest daughter, the first to get married, just told him that she was getting married, and he squashed all happiness of the moment by divulging that he too was getting married… to his mistress.

I pretty much gave up on the conversation, sitting with the phone resting near my ear, alone and defeated. When I couldn't hold back the tears anymore, I interrupted his tale, "Dad, I have to go, a customer just walked in."

"Ok, sweetie, I'll talk to you later. Congrats on the engagement!"

Blinking through blurry tears, I found the "end call" button and went into the backroom to release the sobs caught in my throat.

Disenchanted Bride

I was an easy baby, bald with giant blue eyes that earned compliments from everyone we met. My parents called me baby Yoda because of those same features. I was also nearly hairless until I was a year old when the white-blond curls started forming at my neck.

In middle- and high school, these compliments made me embarrassed of my big eyes; if they're big enough to be noticed, they're *different* and no teenager wants to feel different, even if different was considered beautiful. I started to hate my big eyes and would squint just enough to make them feel like they looked more normal-sized.

I also have freckles over my body, the darker, bigger kind that are technically moles but aren't raised as you think of moles as being. I hated them as a kid, and they made me feel incredibly self-conscious, even though a good friend was so jealous of them that she'd add them to her own face with makeup. Through high school and into college I suffered from acne, only on my face, and would rarely even come to breakfast without make-up on, covering up the little red bumps as best I could. My insecurities have plagued me my entire life, feeling awkward in the skin I was given.

"I hope our kids don't get your lame eye color or shitty skin."

Scott knew of my insecurities, but would "joke" with me about how he hoped our future kids wouldn't be plagued with them as well. In his mind, if he laughed about it, it was only a joke and shouldn't be considered hurtful. If I let him know it upset me, I "couldn't take a joke."

"They better have ocean-blue eyes and clear skin like me." Scott's eyes were blue, with mine being more blue/green/gray that seem to change colors with whatever I'm wearing. To Scott, only the bright blue of his eye color was noteworthy. He also rarely had a pimple and not a freckle or mole to be found. Again, these "jokes" passed as his personality, and while I was offended and hurt, my feelings were never validated but rather I was told to "lighten up, it's just a joke."

Our wedding was planned for the following summer, almost a year and a half after we got engaged. Planning the wedding was fairly effortless. He had known since high school that he wanted to have his wedding reception at the same place he'd had his senior prom. I had never given much thought about my someday wedding, so I was more than okay with his choice of venue.

Scott's family was Catholic, and I knew it was important to him and his family that we get married in a church. Not being religious myself, if I was going to be married in a church, I wanted it to be the most beautiful church around – the Cathedral of St. Paul.

This church was built in the early 1900s as the tallest building in St. Paul, Minnesota, on the highest hill in the area. It was built to be seen. The massive exterior is made from local, light-gray granite bricks, capped by a gigantic copper dome which creates a nearly 200-foot ceiling inside.

We toured the church before booking our ceremony, and as soon as I walked in, I exclaimed, "Now *this* is a church!"

Mom was with us on the tour and she laughed at my exclamation because it was so unexpected. Of *course* this was a church, but I hadn't expected to love it so much. Scott just smiled in a way that said, "This'll do!"

Mom grew up Catholic, going to parochial school until high school, so most of what I learned about the religion was from her, which wasn't much at all. I'd been with Scott and his family a few times over the years, but it was always uncomfortable for me. I didn't know when to stand or kneel or what the prayers were, and Scott seemed embarrassed to have me there with him because I didn't know those things.

"Just come up with me to take communion. No one will know or care that you're not Catholic." He'd say.

"I would know, and your family would know, and I'm fairly certain your God would know." I remained seated in the pew alone while I watched them make their way up to the priest and back.

For some reason, being there for my wedding didn't have the same stigma about it for me. The church was a place to hold the ritual of our ceremony, not the place of worship it was during a mass. It had a rich architectural history that reminded me of churches I'd toured in London while on a school trip to visit the fashion houses for a college course. Stained glass windows spread colored light throughout the airy, solid, columned interior. The sound of our shoes as we walked down the aisle echoed hauntingly, and I thought, "This place makes my soul feel at one with the heavens."

The seating capacity at the Cathedral is 3,000, and I felt dwarfed knowing we would not be inviting even a tenth of that. I tried to imagine myself walking down that aisle, our friends and family filling only the first half of the rows of pews surrounding the aisle, my face unable to stop grinning, both from nervousness and excitement. This was the first time I'd envisioned myself walking down an aisle to get married and I was both excited and terrified. *Was this really happening?*

I could smell the incense from the service earlier in the day and wondered if they would use that during our ceremony too. Since I didn't know much about what to expect from the church experience, I didn't have any expectations. "Just tell me where to be and what I need to do when."

Outside of finding the perfect church, I didn't have many requirements for our wedding. My favorite color was purple, so that was our color theme. I wanted simple elegance, and Scott had extravagant ideas, as expected. He said that he wanted Boyz-II-Men to sing at the wedding, or a white horse to walk down the aisle ahead of the bridal party. I laughed at the absurdity of it all because I couldn't even imagine such flair at *our* wedding! It sounded like something you'd see in a celebrity magazine, or for Hollywood royalty that could afford such extravagance. I do not like attention drawn to me, and a wedding itself is enough attention.

I knew that I wanted a timeless wedding dress, a classic, full of lace and beads. I didn't want it to be stark white, because I wasn't "virgin white" material. It was important to me for my dress to be some form of off-white without being ivory. Not being the religious type myself, if I was to be getting married in *the* cathedral, I figured I should respect their beliefs.

When it came time to go dress shopping, I couldn't; I became too nervous - like none of it felt real and the endless choices in wedding dresses were overwhelming. I didn't know who to bring with me to the bridal salon to help me try on and decide on the perfect dress. I knew this was something women typically brought friends, moms, and sisters to, but I was used to doing things on my own and I hated shopping with other people, preferring to shop without the help of a salesperson or any shopping partners.

I went to a couple of dress shops by myself to test the waters, just flipping through the dresses on the racks, occasionally trying one or two on in the fitting room. I felt silly and embarrassed in the fitting room alone. I didn't feel beautiful, and I didn't feel excited. I quickly got dressed and put everything back; I just wasn't doing the whole wedding planning thing right. It was so unnatural for me and something I just hadn't given much thought to.

A girlfriend convinced me to go to a bridal show for some ideas, mostly just to try to get me excited about the process. With all of the options examples laid out in front of me, it finally started to feel more real, and I decided that I could do this. While at the bridal show, we found an ad for a small bridal boutique near downtown, and I called to make an appointment. I asked Mom if she would come with me, mostly because I knew that was the expectation for a girl getting married, but also because I wanted someone there with me.

She and my sixteen-year-old sister met me at the boutique, excited to be a part of the day.

"I'm surprised you invited us." Mom said when they got there. She knew I was mostly independent and hadn't asked her to go shopping with me since before I could drive myself.

"I know, but I think my *mom* should be here with me when I'm trying on *wedding* dresses!" I replied, realizing that I did want her there and that I was needing her support through the process. I hadn't talked with her about the wedding planning much at all because I knew it wasn't her thing and she wouldn't feel comfortable trying to help. She knew I had an "eye" for planning and left me to it.

Since I had my dress type narrowed down, there were only a few for me to try on. Mom and my sister sat in the designated "guest" chairs placed in front of the platform where I was to stand and see myself in full 360-degrees while rotating in front of the wall of mirrors. I came out of the fitting room, shyly at first, gathering the long, heavy fabric in my hands so that I could step up to the platform. I picked the one I liked the least to try on first, just to get it out of the way, wanting to make sure that it didn't happen to look differently once on. It didn't, so I was comfortable in my original opinion. I looked like a barbie inside a cupcake and it was not the look I was hoping for.

After debating between two great contenders, I asked my spectators to help me decide on the winner. The dress itself had a name, Jorie Ann, and that was the deciding factor. Jorie was the name of a college classmate and I had loved her name, thinking that I might one day name my future daughter that. Ann is my middle name, as it is the middle name for all of the women on Mom's side ahead of me. If I did have a daughter, her middle name would've also been Ann, so it seemed like fate was helping me choose my wedding dress.

It was a strapless dress, in the most perfect not-quite-white shade, with a full overlay of lace and beads running the entire length of the dress, train and all. It was fitted, not quite mermaid style, but enough to accentuate my waist and hips, with fabric buttons lining the back. I knew the church would require me to cover my shoulders, so I needed to also find a veil. I loved the dress so much and didn't want to cover it up with an intricate veil, but we found a simple and sheer, long veil to match the length of the train. I tried it on with the dress and suddenly had to fight back tears. For the first time, I felt happy rather than awkward and embarrassed. This was real, and I was getting married!

In the few years leading up to our wedding, Jessica Simpson and Nick Lachey had gotten married and she had put out a few wedding planning books that I scooped up and read with abandon. Their TV show *Newlyweds* was something Scott and I would watch together, feeling like we were couple-twins with them, as their relationship was just like ours. Not surprisingly, I idolized her and wanted to look as beautiful as she did on her wedding day. Unintentionally, our dresses were remarkably similar.

She had thick, long hair that she wore loosely curled, down around her shoulders. I wanted the same. My sister Marie's best friend was a hairstylist, so I scheduled her to do my hair the day of the wedding. She had been highlighting and cutting my hair for a few years already, so she was familiar with my hair and its quirky tendencies. I asked her to put extensions in beforehand so that I could have the long, full look that I hoped for. It was the first time I'd ever had extensions, and I thoroughly enjoyed having twice as much hair! You long-haired girls are lucky; I have very fine hair that doesn't look nice past shoulder length.

Our groom's dinner was the night before the wedding, which was a dinner boat cruise with our wedding party and families. Our parents were there, including Dad and his new wife, and Mom with Kent, the man she'd been dating for a couple of years by then. Kent offered to bring his quartet band to play during the cocktail hour before our wedding reception, which Scott and I were excited about, and I appreciated how much he loved and cared for Mom.

For the boat cruise, I wore a calf-length, flowy off-white dress with pleats, summoning my inner Marilyn Monroe in the dress billowing scene, especially when the wind picked up on the lake. Scott wore typical boat attire, blue chinos with a white button-up and deck shoes. We ate and drank the evening away, and everyone was happy and excited for the following day's events.

We had decided we didn't want to see each other until I walked down the aisle to marry him, so at the end of the night

Scott went to stay at one of the groomsman's houses, and I went back to our house with some of the bridesmaids. I laid in bed that night with no sign of sleep to come. My mind was racing but not because I was nervous about the wedding itself. Would Scott be hungover in the morning? He often struggled to call it a night, suffering from the fear-of-missing-out syndrome. Was he going to be staying where he said he was? Were they going to a strip club? What if he had the pre-wedding jitters and they decided to bring home strippers? Something seemed a bit out of place for it being the night before our wedding.

Scott had a way of making me feel insecure about his behavior, without anything ever being outright obvious to me. I was thinking back to Angie, the "drug friend," and how I knew deep down that their time with each other wasn't as innocent as he had claimed. There had been other moments during our early dating years that I shouldn't have overlooked—like the time a girl from his work called me at my parent's house to tell me that Scott was also seeing her friend. When I had answered the phone, I thought it was a joke, like the prank calls I'd gotten when working as the cashier at the car dealership.

"I just thought you should know that Scott has been dating Rachel for a few weeks now. We thought you guys broke up, but it doesn't sound like that's the case." Why would she think we broke up? How did she know where I lived to get my phone number? A million questions raced through my mind but all I could do was react. I was so upset with him, and her, I ran down the stairs, throwing the necklace he gave me across the room. Mom listened to me sob out the story, and when I was done, suggested that everyone deserves to tell their side of the story.

I believed him when he told me that this girl at work was "crazy" and had always looked to start drama. He said the girl who called me had a crush on him and was bitter that he didn't like her too, so she was looking for revenge. I brushed off the joke he made about how he hadn't cheated on me "since we'd been

60

engaged." Had he been telling me the truth all along, but covered it with so much sarcasm to make it seem implausible?

The morning of our wedding was a somewhat dreary June day with a chance of sprinkles on and off; rain on your wedding day is supposed to bring good luck, right? I must've gotten some semblance of sleep because I woke up smiling, knowing *this was the day*. The bridesmaids all came over for mimosas and to do each other's hair and makeup as we had decided it would be more intimate and fun to have everyone get ready at my house rather than pay a salon to do the same. The kitchen counters were strewn with makeup bags, curling irons, and curlers of various sizes. We did pinned-back curls rather than complicated up-dos, and everyone felt pretty comfortable doing their own makeup or getting help from one of the other girls.

I had an image in my head of what I wanted to look like for my big day, and I did my best to convey it to my girls. Hair down in loose, long curls, with the sides pinned up to give the half-up effect; simple makeup, highlighting my eyes with smokey shadow and dark mascara. While I was being pampered, I felt beautiful, and the girls did everything they could to gush on me and make me feel special. This was my wedding day, the day so many women look forward to.

Getting ready took more time than we'd allotted for, and we needed to finish up and get going. I walked into the bathroom to see the final effect, staring at myself in the mirror, not recognizing the person looking back at me.

"I thought I was going to look beautiful." the voice in my head said.

I looked at this woman in the mirror seeing that she had the hair and makeup I had asked for, but she wasn't what I expected to see.

"You can still see the acne bumps." I thought, grabbing more makeup to cover them up.

"Why isn't my hair falling as I expected it to?" Tears pooled in my eyes and I had to fight them off so they wouldn't ruin the work that had been done.

I was alone in the bathroom and I hated the way I saw myself in the mirror. I did not feel like a beautiful bride, and I wanted to take it all off and start again. But I couldn't; we were now running late, and we needed to pack up to drive to the church. I blotted away my tears, telling myself *there's nothing I can do now*, and it just is what it is. I didn't tell the girls how I felt, I couldn't; they would've just tried to make me feel better because that's what friends do.

"You look just like Jessica Simpson!" Lacey gushed.

"So beautiful." Emily agreed.

I had seen what I looked like and I did not agree with them, but still, I responded with a polite, "Thank you!"

I assured myself that I would do what I could to fix it once I got to the church.

We packed our dresses and bags and piled into the cars to drive thirty minutes to the church. Once there, we made our way to the bridal room where we began the final process of getting ready to walk down the aisle. The photographer, my cousin Grace, was there waiting for us, and I panicked inside knowing that I wasn't happy with the way I looked.

"I have to try to fix myself first!" I thought, ducking out of the way so she wouldn't take pictures of me yet.

Grace started snapping in-the-moment pictures of the girls, my wedding dress on the hanger, while I made my way over to the mirror along the wall. How could I *discreetly* fix myself? I hadn't told anyone I was unhappy with the way I looked, and Lacey had done exactly what I asked her to, how could I let them know I didn't like it? We didn't have much time before needing to be in our places and I didn't want the girls to notice that I was stressed.

I grabbed my makeup bag and started dabbing and powdering where I could, trying not to overdo it. Using my fingers to lightly comb through the curls, I realized that this was just how I look. This was what I looked like all made up, and regardless of the image I had in my head, this was the result and there was nothing I could do about it now. I forced a smile at myself in the mirror, pushing the disappointment down, and turned to have the girls help me get into my beautiful dress.

Dad walked me down the aisle, as is tradition. We stood outside of the closed doors that led into the cavernous church, the rest of the bridal party waiting in front of us. Watching the bridesmaids and groomsmen couple off and walk down the aisle in front of us was surreal. I felt like I was watching someone else's wedding, not my own. I was so terrified to walk down that aisle with everyone staring at me, my heart was jumping in my chest, the blood whooshing through my ears, and my whole body sweating while waiting for the doors to open for us to walk through.

I put my arm through Dad's and thought that he was supposed to make me feel comforted, to alleviate my nervous energy, but that comfort didn't come from him. I felt shaky and nervous but didn't want to cause my dad to worry. He seemed nervous too, but we stood there with each other, in near silence.

Finally, the doors opened, and it was our turn to walk down the endless aisle to the altar, where I would be handed over to my groom to say, "I do." Even though my dad and I were walking down the aisle together, I felt as though I was walking alone, staring straight ahead to my soon-to-be husband, eager to get there in hopes of finding comfort in his hands. When we finally got there, Dad started to bring my arm towards Scott's, passing the baton, but then pulled back quickly, pretending that he wasn't going to give me up. We all laughed, which lifted the anxiety nearly crushing my chest.

Once I was standing next to Scott, I felt comforted, knowing that he would know what to do. Standing there in the church was an incredibly unfamiliar environment for me, and I looked to him to help me navigate our world. I don't remember what he said to me at that moment. I like to think that he told me I looked beautiful, but the truth is, I'm not sure if he would have. "Great" maybe, but not beautiful. There were too many times I'd been told something looked amiss for him to suddenly start telling me I looked perfect.

If you've ever been to a Catholic wedding, you know that they are long and full of ceremony. Scott and I stood at the front of the altar for some time while the priest read bible verses and gave a speech. He was Scott's family's priest from their hometown church, a guest priest at the cathedral, and he had stories to tell. After a while, we were moved to giant velvet chairs just off to the side of the altar that almost felt fit for a king and queen. My legs were grateful for the chance to be sitting down, even if just for a bit before being summoned back to the pulpit. While we had practiced all of this the night before, it hadn't included all of the speakers and singers and prayers, so I truly had no idea how long we would be up there. I think I started to daydream a few times, and most of the ceremony is a blur in my memory.

Finally, we said our vows and "I dos", which were ceremonious and formal, and it was announced that we were now husband and wife, able to seal the deal with a kiss. Scott tried to make a show with the kiss, bending me backward and making it last longer than it should have been, but we finally made our way back up the aisle with beaming smiles while our guests cheered us on. I was so relieved for it to be over! This time, I didn't care that everyone was looking at me. They were there to celebrate us and their smiles were contagious.

After the wedding was the reception at the place Scott had his senior prom. It was a beautiful open room with marble floors, a double staircase leading to the dinner tables and dancefloor, with walls of windows surrounding it all. We began with a cocktail hour, serenaded by my mom's "pseudo spouse's" string-quartet band, followed by dinner and dancing.

I chose "Somewhere Over the Rainbow" by Israel Kamakawi-wo'ole for our father-daughter dance, because it felt like a song my dad sang to me when I was little. I didn't want to stand out and I *very much* disliked being the center of attention that I considered skipping this dance altogether. Instead, we combined the mother-son and father-daughter dance just so I didn't have to be out there alone, all eyes on me. To this day my dad will occasionally send me a text with a link to that song, his way of letting me know that he's thinking about me and remembering our dance fondly.

When Scott determined our presence was no longer needed at our reception, we slipped out quietly, only notifying the best man that we were headed out. We had booked a room at an expensive hotel downtown, about fifteen minutes away from the reception, and we were exhausted from the long day so we were excited to get checked in.

"May I have your ID please?" The woman dressed in all black asked Scott.

We stood in front of the lobby's stark and modern check-in counter, confronted with a request for an ID to prove we were the actual bride and groom who had reserved the room for the night. Scott felt around for his wallet, unsuccessfully.

"I must've left my wallet back at the reception," Scott said, looking at me for a solution.

"We just came from our reception and neither of us has our ID. What else can we do?" I tried to plead with the woman behind the counter.

"Is there someone that could fax us a copy of your driver's license?" she offered.

FAX? Who would have access to a fax machine at this time, if ever? Since we had not been responsible for our belongings at all that day, we had not realized neither one of us had our driver's license or any credit cards. It was after midnight, and even though we were dressed in a wedding gown and tuxedo, we were not going to be granted access to our room.

Finally accepting defeat, we took our bags and drove the thirty-five minutes back home. Exhausted and annoyed by the evening's turn of events, we plopped into bed, falling asleep still wearing our wedding attire.

It's a Baby

A few months before the wedding, I ran out of money to keep my store afloat. I had to close the doors and file for bankruptcy. I felt like such a failure, and I was embarrassed about both, closing the store and declaring bankruptcy. That's what I had gone to school for, and what I loved doing. What was I going to do now? I still didn't want to work for a big corporation like Target, and I knew a typical retail job wouldn't be the 9-5 job I wanted.

Scott suggested I work for him as an admin or office manager, which seemed like the best option at the time; it gave me the freedom to work on wedding projects or run to various appointments. He was making enough money to support us, and if I could help him be more organized and efficient, why not? This allowed us to be together nearly constantly, which both of us enjoyed at first.

However, shortly after the wedding, we decided that I should find a real job to bring in an income and provide us both with proper health insurance. I found a job surprisingly quickly based on the recommendation of an acquaintance, a business analyst in procurement for a large financial company downtown. I was going to be working for a large corporation after all. It was all new to me, as the only jobs I'd ever had were in a retail setting. Now I was expected to wear a badge and sit at a desk in a cubical all day, which sounded somewhat tortuous, but doable.

One month after starting my new job, the night before New Year's Eve, I was getting into bed when Scott asked, "Hey, weren't you supposed to get your period today?"

The question surprised me because I had no idea that Scott paid attention to my menstrual cycle enough to pinpoint a specific day where I would or wouldn't get my period. It was true; I should've gotten it that day as it almost always started on a Sunday afternoon, like clockwork. I hadn't put any thought into it, this was my first month off the pill and I had no idea how my body would react. We weren't trying to get pregnant; I just started a new job and was waiting for insurance to kick in on January 1st before I could get my new prescription. I had been crampy all day and just assumed my period would start soon. I never gave it any additional thought.

The morning came and we decided to go to the science museum to pass the time. Every time I'd go to the bathroom Scott would ask, "Did you get it yet?"

And as the day went on, we both started to question whether or not my period would actually come. While walking around the museum, he told me to jump up and down the stairs, hoping that that would get my period started. We laughed about it, both because it would be funny to start hopping up and down the stairs, but also because we were scared that it hadn't come yet and what that would mean. We had not talked about starting a family, and honestly, after being on the pill for ten years straight, I never thought I would get pregnant so quickly. I'd heard plenty of people say they tried for months after going off the pill. I hadn't even learned how to perform my new job yet, and I was worried about having to do that while my body dealt with being pregnant for the first time.

As we left the museum to head home, we decided we should probably stop at the pharmacy to pick up a pregnancy test. We were scheduled to go to a New Year's Eve party at the neighbor's house later that night and I needed to know if it would be ok to have some drinks.

Scott pulled up to the pharmacy and sent me in to buy the test. I walked into the store, feeling somewhat nervous, somewhat excited, and very embarrassed. The *only* item I had to buy was a pregnancy test. They didn't have self-checkout counters then, so the cashier would know exactly what I was going to be doing. I wondered whether he would wish me luck, whichever way I wanted it to go, or if he felt embarrassed too, knowing that we were sharing this moment of "what will it say?"

I wondered if he'd give me another thought later, pondering what the result of that test was.

Scott waited for me in the car, and as the automatic doors opened when I walked out of the store, the song "Bittersweet Symphony" by The Verve started playing in the car. Scott said that, at that moment, he knew the test would be positive, and that I was pregnant.

The news itself would be bittersweet, exciting but scary at the same time. We were both nervous the rest of the ride home, not saying much. I remember trying not to smile from my nerves because I wasn't quite sure how I felt. I had wanted to have kids my whole life, but at this moment, I felt completely unprepared. Wasn't this something that you spent time discussing and planning? Aren't you supposed to get a couple of negatives before trying again the next month?

We finally got home, and I immediately headed to the bathroom off the kitchen to pee on the stick. Once done, I walked into the kitchen and set the test on the counter to wait the required two minutes. Scott set the timer on the microwave and we stood there, chatting about anything but the impending result. At the sound of the *ding* from the timer, I reached for the stick, quickly read the result, and burst into tears.

It was positive! Scott wrapped his arms around me saying, "Holy shit!" over and over. We were both crying real, happy tears; we were excited for this and we knew it was going to be great. Exactly one month into my new job, on New Year's Eve, we found out I was pregnant.

The NYE party was still on, and we still planned to attend, however, we had this secret that we were not prepared to tell anyone yet. I spent the night drinking 7-up with a splash of grenadine or cranberry juice just so that it looked like I was partaking, sparing either of us the premature declaration that we were expecting a baby. Thankfully, no one noticed, and we ended the night just after the countdown to midnight. What a way to start a year!

Pregnancy was easy for me, and I enjoyed every minute of it. I had always assumed that I'd be plagued with morning sickness because I suffer from extreme motion sickness, but I only felt a little queasy once on the bus to work. I'm not sure why I related the two, but I just figured if I get nauseous easily, it would be worse while pregnant.

I was still working downtown and had started taking the bus to work so that I could get a nap in after work. The first time I felt the baby kick was on a quiet morning ride while it was still dark outside. I had my eyes closed, my hands resting on my barely protruding belly when I felt the smallest flutter inside. At first, I thought it was a muscle spasm or something, but then I realized I had felt my baby move. My cheeks flushed as I smiled because the grin was an involuntary reaction to the love bursting inside me.

Another woman on my team at work was also pregnant with her first, only a month or so further along than me. We had similar views on parenting and spent a lot of time sharing our pregnancy's ups and downs. It was fun to have someone to share the experience with, especially since I was also still learning the job. We took walks over lunch, visiting the nearby baby boutiques and clothing stores, both of us shopping gender-neutrally. We did not find out the sex of the baby, so we were anxiously awaiting to find out if it was a boy or a girl. Scott was positive it would be a girl since there are so many in my family, but I just felt he was a boy the whole pregnancy. I was drawn to boy's clothes, names, and toys, almost as if I knew I was having a boy.

During my pregnancy, autism awareness seemed to be booming and information on the topic was everywhere, whether it was factual or not. Scare tactics work wonders on a first-time pregnant mama, and I was determined to do everything I could to prevent my child from having autism. I tried to eat organic and clean as much as a craving pregnant woman could. I switched to all-natural cleaning and skin-care products, eliminating as much artificial crap from my life as I could, and focused on being serene in my pregnancy.

Scott was supportive during pregnancy, reading through baby name books with me and fantasizing about what life would look like once the baby arrived. He wasn't necessarily excited though. Because I'd had the store and was passionate about all things baby, he looked to me for guidance on things we'd need and how to prepare for a baby to join our twosome. He truly had no clue what it meant to take care of a baby or what birth entailed and didn't care to learn too much about it, either. He'd laugh at my nesting routine of vacuuming the walls of the nursery but would walk around the neighborhood with me in hopes to get labor started.

Our baby was due, not unironically, on Labor Day, September 7. We have several birthdays in our family that fall on the same month/day combo, August 8th, for example, so when September 7 came and went, I asked my doctor if I could be induced for the baby to be born on 9/9. My doctor assured me that, while overdue, my baby just wasn't ready to be born yet, and she would not schedule the induction as requested. She opted for the 14th instead, one week past due.

Finally, one day before I was to be induced, I started having contractions. They were certainly not consistent, and not too intense, but for a first-time mama, any progress is exciting. The contractions continued throughout the day, on and off, and eventually through the night as well. Sunday morning came around and they were still random and not reliable, so I told Scott he should play in the golf tournament he was scheduled for. The tournament was on our home course, so he wouldn't be too far away should things progress. The induction was scheduled for 8 pm that night and we had plenty of time until then.

It was a dreary and drizzly day, and I remember lying in our bed watching the movie *Penelope*. The movie was fairly new, starring Christina Ricci; she is born with a pig's snout for a nose and grows up to try to find true love to accept her as she is. It was a decent movie to watch while passing the time laboring, even if it did make me question whether my baby would be born with any animal features.

Scott was able to play the whole tournament, but deciding it might be pushing it too much to stay for the dinner reception afterward, he came home to see my progress. While he was gone, the contractions had gotten much closer together and they were now consistently three to five minutes apart. The hospital called just then, asking if we could come in earlier for the induction since they had room for us, and I said that I was already in labor and we were on our way anyway.

Labor was hard, and Scott had no idea how to support me. I had mistakenly thought the nurses would be there to help me throughout my labor, but they only stopped in periodically to check vitals and symptoms. This was the same hospital at which I had job shadowed ten years earlier, so I should've known that the nurses came in to hold your legs while pushing, but that was about it. I had taken doula courses, nursing classes, birthing classes, and read countless books and websites, but none of it prepared me for an unsupported birth experience.

I tried walking the halls with Scott while also trying to talk to Mom on the phone to give her an update; I didn't want anyone at the hospital with us because I thought it would stress me out. I had gone into the labor process thinking I would go as long as possible without pain meds, but that ended up being only about an hour after arriving at the hospital. The nurse had just given me something to relax when Mom and my sister Christine showed up. They just couldn't help themselves and were so excited. The medication left me loopy. I felt warm and comfortable, however, I couldn't carry on a conversation in the least, so they left and agreed they'd come back once the baby was born.

Eventually, I received an epidural and was able to rest for several hours into the night. The nurse came in to check on me and let me know it was time to start pushing – leg holding time! It didn't go well. I was into my third day of labor and I was exhausted. The nurses were holding my legs up while I pushed, Scott at my head staring at the wall behind my head, unable to be a part of the action between my legs. The baby's heart rate kept dropping with each contraction and the nurses were getting nervous. I was getting nervous too, remembering my internship and having to yell "CODE" because something was happening with the baby. I didn't know what was happening then and I didn't know what was happening now. The doctor came in, which was not the doctor I'd been seeing throughout my pregnancy, and he tried to assure me that everything was ok but that we needed to get the baby out quickly. After several pushes, the doctor used the vacuum to assist the delivery, and baby was born quickly and safely.

Our baby boy, Joey, ended up being born on the morning of

September 15, eight days past his due date. Any amount of time past one's due date feels like a cruel punishment after looking forward to that date for nine months! He had a cone-shaped bruise on the back of his head from the vacuum, but he was otherwise flawless.

After Joey was born, they took him to the nursery to monitor him in case he had inhaled any meconium, which is a baby's first poop, since there was meconium in the amniotic fluid. They held him up so I could see him, and I remember looking at him across the room thinking he was so long and skinny, alien-like. He was 7 lbs, 6 oz, 22 inches long, and absolutely perfect. I didn't get to hold him for a while after he was born, but Scott followed him to the nursery. He later told me that he was so scared during the delivery that he prayed for God to keep me and the baby safe, that he would start going to church on Sundays if everything turned out ok. I didn't know he was a praying man, and he hadn't gone to church much over the previous few years, but I was surprised at his willingness to share his emotions and it felt like such an intimate moment.

Scott went home after Joey and I were settled in the postpartum room, hoping to get some real sleep in our bed. I loved being able to spend the alone time, just my new baby and me, and everything came naturally for the two of us together. He was a great nurser from the start, and it all seemed so effortless.

Not Just a Boy

Joey was a content baby; he ate well, was happy, and overall, a wonderful baby for new parents. Except he didn't sleep, and he seemed to have endless energy. I had three younger sisters, and my family just didn't know much about what little boys were like, so I didn't have anything to compare him to. We were visiting my dad for dinner one night, and I had gone upstairs to nurse Joey. He was about two months old and had always been a great eater, and we'd never had any problems nursing. But this time, something was bothering Joey and he wouldn't eat, arching his back away and screaming. I tried different positions, but nothing was working. I got so worked up and thought something must have certainly been wrong.

I brought him down to the kitchen where Dad and Scott were chatting. Handing Joey to my dad I said, "I don't know what's wrong with him! He won't stop crying and he will not eat. This has never happened to us before!"

I was scared and trying not to cry, asking my doctor-dad for any sort of help or advice.

Dad's response was, "What do you want me to do?" while gently bouncing Joey in his arms.

Scott just laughed at me, "I'm sure he'll be fine, go try again."

Realizing I wasn't going to get anywhere with them, I went back upstairs to the spare bedroom and laid Joey on the bed while I cried alongside him. After a few minutes, I wiped away my tears, picked him up, and got him latched on for a normal nursing session.

On our drive home that night, Scott scolded me, "Don't you ever act like that again, it was embarrassing."

He was referring to my asking him and my dad for help, that my need for assistance was embarrassing to him. It was these moments that, over time, taught me not to ask for help.

I can only remember two times when Joey fell asleep on his own as a baby, and one of those times was when my mom was babysitting. He would sit and play, bouncing to his own beat in his bouncy seat, smiling away, but he would never fall asleep.

To get him to fall asleep he needed to bounce, a soothing technique that only grew in intensity as he got older. For the first few months, we could get by holding him upright on our shoulders while lightly bending and straightening our knees to bounce him. By a year he would push himself up and down with his feet on your lap, needing the extra stimulation while we rocked him.

It got hard to hold him like that in the rocking chair, so we moved to a yoga ball where we could get a bigger bounce. We would sit on that ball, bouncing with him, for sometimes up to an hour or more before he finally fell asleep. Getting him to sleep was not a quick and easy process. For naps, I'd often drive around just so he'd sleep, and I got intimately familiar with the back roads of the surrounding towns.

That yoga ball became an integral part of Joey's bedtime and nap routine. The babysitters knew to use it and knew that it could sometimes take an hour of bouncing before he'd fall asleep. We'd take the ball with us when we'd know we would be somewhere else during his nap.

We went away to a cabin with Scott's parents for a weekend

and brought the ball with us there. I sat alone in the bedroom for what felt like hours, coaxing Joey to sleep, while everyone else had happy hour and played family games around the table. If he woke in the middle of the night, I'd quickly jump out of bed to bounce him back to sleep to not wake Scott. At home, I had the buffer of a closed-door in another room to separate our middle-of-the-night wake-up sessions. Scott could not be bothered to be woken up during the night.

There was one particularly tough night on that trip. I was so exhausted from bouncing Joey in the middle of the night, that I was trying to bounce as high as I could while choking back the tears of frustration. Scott woke up to see me bouncing, and nearly yelled, "What the hell are you doing?"

He was berating me for bouncing "too high" with our baby while he lay comfortably in bed. He didn't offer to take a turn, only told me to not be so "crazy" with our child.

I thought that parenting shouldn't be this difficult and that my son had to be more than "just a boy."

I heard that so often, "Oh, he's just a boy! They're like that. They have endless energy, and they are very curious." I just didn't know what to do about it. I knew I was struggling, but hearing it was "normal" only made me question my abilities as a mother.

I went back to work after maternity leave, and my sister, Christine, became his nanny until he was about nine months old. She's my baby sister and was only nineteen years old at the time. She didn't quite know what she wanted to do with her life yet, so she had free time. Joey and Christine got along great. They didn't have a care in the world except to hang out and have fun. I loved that he got to be at home, and I loved that I had my sister there to care for him.

But after only a few months, I wasn't sleeping at night, and working full-time at a corporate job downtown just wasn't working for our family. Scott couldn't manage taking care of Joey until my sister got there in the mornings, often texting me frantically and eventually angrily about whatever he was struggling with. He'd say, "He just pooped, and I have no idea how to get his shirt off," or "he won't take the bottle and he's crying." Scott was so used to having me or Christine take care of Joey that he had no idea how to do it himself.

I would get frustrated because I was on a bus to work and couldn't just turn around to come home and take care of it, which is exactly what he'd wanted me to do; he wanted to be relieved of the task of parenting immediately. I felt anxious all the time, his outbursts making me feel inadequate, always needing to fix something. We talked about having me quit work to stay home, but Scott also didn't want us to lose my income. He coached me to have a meeting with my manager to let him know that I got a job offer elsewhere, for 50% more than I was currently making, to see if they'd match the offer. This seemed ridiculous to me; it was a flat-out lie. However, Scott always seemed to be successful in business, and I thought he must know what he's doing and how to get ahead. I also didn't feel like I had a choice; Scott's suggestions were not merely proposals, they were demands.

I scheduled the meeting, had the conversation, and it went as I'd expected. "Ok then, well, congratulations on a great opportunity! But we are unable to match that offer to have you stay."

So, I quit, and became the stay-at-home mom I had always wanted to be. I was thrilled to have this opportunity. I was excited knowing I would wake up to his sweet face and be able to spend the whole day with him, bonding, and learning about the world together. I made homemade meals and made a point of introducing all kinds of different flavors and textures so that he would not be a picky eater. He'd squish all the food through his fingers and smash it on his tray, shoveling it all in excitedly. When we went outside for walks, he could not be contained by a stroller and just had to experience the world with his own hands and feet.

Though I was getting to fulfill my dream of being a stay-at-home mama, raising my babe, it was a lot of work, and not everything was exactly as I had dreamed. Joey was so busy and required so much attention that I couldn't do anything else in my day except try to keep him occupied and safe. His favorite activities consisted of being outside, carrying armfuls of dad's tools: screwdrivers, hammers, the leaf blower, and anything else his toddler hands could grasp, and tinkering by himself. He did not want to interact through play but preferred to maintain his own agenda and figure stuff out by himself.

I wanted to do art projects and read books and play games together, but it seemed like all I did was follow him around or sit and watch him play by himself. He would chew books, or flip through the pages without ever looking at them. If we tried to do a painting project, he would paint his face instead of the paper in front of him. If it were too cold outside, we'd be inside and he'd still have his screwdrivers and tools, attempting to take off door knobs or drawer pulls. He was fixated on vacuums, "tappums" as he called them, wanting to vacuum nearly every day. Sometimes he would dig the dirt out of the plants just so that we could get out the vacuum.

Joey also liked to carry around a lamp and plug it in and out of as many outlets as he could find. We had outlet covers—the near bulletproof kind that required special tools to remove. But he had those screwdrivers and could whip those outlet covers off in a heartbeat! And so, I spent the majority of my days redirecting his activities and attempting to keep him safe.

By now, my marriage was suffering and I didn't have a supportive spouse. As he had not been involved in much of the parenting duties and did not want to hear about what Joey and I did during the day, Scott only saw all the things I didn't get done for him. I felt pressure to keep a clean house to avoid him pointing out the crumbs on the floor. I mowed the lawn during Joey's nap so that Scott didn't have to do it after work.

Scott didn't think I was doing enough for him or contributing enough to the household by staying home, so I decided to look for a new job. I consistently felt like a disappointment. Again, I found a job quickly, this time as an administrative assistant/financial analyst for a technology company twenty minutes from home. It was another cubicle desk job, but it was closer to home, and I would be working with a sales team instead of procurement, making money for the business rather than spending it.

I felt like a failure. Moms stay home with their kids all the time. Why was it so hard for me? Was I causing him to be so difficult? Was I a terrible parent? When I tried to explain my struggles to others, they tended to think I wanted them to commiserate with me or to tell me there was nothing wrong with my child.

Those were not the right things to say. There doesn't have to be something *wrong* for parenting to be difficult. Providing reassurance *felt* to others like the right thing to do, but to me, the reassurance felt like blame, as though I was somehow the one with the problem.

"Oh, he's just fine! Just a typical boy. There's nothing wrong with him." translates to "You're obviously obsessing, and if this is too hard for you, then maybe you need to figure out how to parent better!"

Obviously, that's extreme and no one actually meant those things when they offered reassurance, but when someone expresses concern about their child—for any reason—they likely have a valid motivation.

When I needed someone to listen, I got advice instead. They'd tell me that nothing was wrong with my child, trying to offer comfort, knowing that no parent wants to have something *wrong* with their kid. But when I'd say something was different or difficult with my child, and be told there was nothing wrong, it only made me feel that I was the one with the problem, that I just didn't know how to do it "right."

Feeling that I had a difficult child, I Googled and researched a heck of a lot. I tried the "tried and true" methods and found over and over that they didn't work for my kid. I got tired of telling people their suggestions didn't work, and I felt like a negative Nancy. Bitterness crept in because *of course* I'd looked into all of that, and hearing other people give me suggestions just started to feel like they didn't believe in me and my ability to help my child.

When I went back to work, we decided to put Joey in a Montessori daycare center close to our house. He had just turned two and was in the toddler room, but by 33 months they moved him up to the 3-year-old room where he was expected to be potty trained. He wasn't even close.

He didn't nap and he had been getting into trouble daily for biting and being disruptive. One day during pick up, I found out that to get him to rest or fall asleep at naptime, one of the teachers would sit with him, her legs over his to hold him down so he could calm down and rest. One would think this would be upsetting to hear, that someone was physically holding my son down to get him to rest. But to be honest, I knew they were doing what they could to help him, as well as keep him from disrupting the rest of the kids.

The Director, Shannon, called me in for a parent meeting to discuss his behavior. "Joey has been struggling with his behavior since we've moved him up with the older kids," she started.

"The other kids are afraid of him because of his biting, and he doesn't seem to understand how to follow directions from the teachers. We are beginning to think this isn't the best fit for him for care."

The pain inside me welled up. I wanted to defend him, but also to admit defeat. I didn't know what to do, and I didn't know how to fix it. I couldn't process why this was all so difficult for me. For us. I'd been around babies and kids my whole life, and I'd wanted nothing more than to be here, in this place in my life as a mom.

Seeing my inner turmoil, Shannon continued, kindly, "Joey seems to be struggling with something more. He isn't just misbehaving like a normal toddler, and he isn't trying to be difficult on purpose."

I started to cry, telling her how awful I had been feeling as a parent, wondering why it was so hard for me and why he was so difficult for me to handle.

Shannon recommended that we have an evaluation done by the school district to see if he would qualify for services through them. Finally, I had *something*. Information. A place to start.

I left her office with mixed emotions; I was relieved that someone agreed with me that he was something "more," but I was also incredibly saddened that my sweet boy was being asked to leave the daycare center due to his behavior. I took him home and smiled at him through my tears.

I contacted the school district right away, and they were able to come to our house within a few days to begin the process of evaluating our son. This was a whole new world of parenting, and I was both excited and terrified to be joining this club. I finally had people I could talk to who would know how to quantify our struggles, but I was terrified because I still had no idea what to expect.

No longer able to return to the Montessori daycare, I had to find somewhere new for Joey. We tried another center, with no luck; he was much too rambunctious for them, and they didn't want to accept him into their care. We tried an in-home daycare where, again, he was taking too much attention from the provider. She also said she could not care for him anymore. We went through five daycare settings in six months before I gave up and hired a nanny.

After a few weeks of evaluations with the school district, it was determined that Joey qualified for services through the school under every category available. The team wanted him to start special education preschool right away, five days a week, to begin teaching him how to communicate and use his motor skills more appropriately.

It was scary to find out that my child had something, but I saw the revelation as an opportunity. Now that I knew what it was called, this "something," I had a starting point, something to grow from. Having a diagnosis meant I could now find tools to help, not only my child but myself as well.

Scott became removed almost entirely from the situation we were in. It was far too painful for him to hear that something was wrong with his child. He knew Joey was busy and an awful lot of work to care for, and he'd already distanced himself from the parenting responsibilities altogether. He wouldn't come to any of the evaluation appointments, didn't want to be a part of the daycare search in any capacity, and was rarely even involved in a pickup or drop-off at daycare. I had understood from the beginning that parenting would fall under my department, but I didn't realize just how one-sided the responsibility became. I was the only one putting in any effort in trying to understand Joey and making daily life more manageable for all of us.

We signed Joey up for the recommended preschool, and he loved it immediately. I loved that we were getting support and information. The school would send a van to our house every morning to pick him up and then bring him home every afternoon. He loved those van drivers and every one of them was a saint; so kind, caring, patient. They seemed to love my boy. At Christmas, and at the end of the school year, they'd give him little gifts: a baseball hat, a toy, just a small gesture to show they cared for him. He still has one of those baseball hats and remembers exactly where and who it came from. He remembers them fondly.

Once we saw how well Joey was doing in the preschool program, I decided to have him medically evaluated to see what more we could do for him. Again, Joey and I met with a team of people, similar to what the school district offered, spending weeks driving forty-five minutes to and from the clinic, meeting with various specialists.

At the final results meeting, we were presented with a list of diagnoses, opening an entirely new category to our language, *disorder*.

Sensory Processing *Disorder*. Receptive and Expressive Language *Disorder*. Motor Planning Development *Disorder*. Sleep Onset *Disorder*. Autism. It was everything I had tried so hard to avoid during pregnancy. Here it was anyway. Autism. But knowing what was making parenting so hard immediately made it so much easier! Giving our struggles a name, something we could work with, gave me relief.

Years later, I sat at my computer and reminisced on just how far we'd come with my boy. I searched to find the email for Shannon, the Director of the Montessori school and thanked her for telling me that it wasn't my fault. I thanked her for helping me, for letting me know we could seek help. I let her know about all the help we'd been receiving and how well he had advanced. She responded quickly, remembering us, and thanked *me* for accepting her information and for not arguing "there's nothing wrong with my child," as parents so often do.

Being in denial isn't helpful for anyone involved. I am a huge advocate of seeking help from professionals if something just doesn't seem right. I have found that it is okay to listen to those professionals even if there didn't appear to be a problem. It was okay to be open to feedback. Nothing they said meant that I was a bad parent, or that something was *wrong* with my child.

As I'm writing this, I notice certain words, such as *I, we,* or *us...*

When I say *we,* I mean the collective we: myself, my son, our helpers. I do not mean Scott and me, as the parents of our son. Because the simple fact is, I did all of this on my own; it was *me* who sought out various evaluations, consultations, and therapies for our son, not *us*.

I did this because I trusted that the experts knew more than I did and that their recommendations came from a specialized skill set. I trusted that they had trained for situations like ours, and I knew they could help Joey. Scott wanted nothing to do with the doctors and therapists, nor the hours and hours of endless paperwork and clinic visits. He didn't want to hear that there was something wrong with his child, so he pretended the issues didn't exist. This also meant that he avoided any of the parenting responsibilities, as Joey was far too difficult for him to understand or manage.

He repeatedly said things like, "It makes me too sad to hear about it," or "poor guy."

Scott felt pity for his son rather than a desire to help him succeed. He felt so sad about his son's struggles that he couldn't even stand to hear about them.

Ghosted

At the same time we received news that Joey needed extra help, we had just found out I was pregnant with our second child. I was terrified of bringing a new baby home with how difficult it was with just one three-year-old. Would it be the same, would this one be just as difficult? How would I possibly manage to spend so much time and energy on the first with a new baby in tow? How would he behave with a new baby around? I shared these concerns with his teachers, and they were so kind and gentle with us as they helped guide us through the transition.

At some point after we had Joey, we started talking about whether we should have another. Scott's answer was always, "Why would anyone have more than one?"

The reality of having children meant there was less time and attention focused on him. Take attention away from a narcissist, and the world as they know it becomes a miserable place to be. Part of the definition of a narcissist is that they are unable to love anyone but themselves. Imagine them as a parent, expected to love their children unconditionally. It just doesn't happen. Sure, they can love the idea of having a child, but mostly as a show for others, since having children is something you *do* after you get married.

Becoming pregnant a second time happened much the same as the first. I had stopped taking the pill and missed my period that first month. We had not talked about any specific timing for another but thought we would just see what happened. It was the afternoon, and for some reason, we had been arguing in the kitchen with Joey running around between us. I had used the same bathroom to pee on the stick as the first time around, setting the pregnancy test back on the counter where the first one had sat three years earlier. We continued to argue, and when the timer was up, I picked up the stick and shouted, "Well, there ya have it, I'm pregnant anyway."

The following events were unmemorable, and we just continued with our daily lives, except that I was now pregnant.

Scott kept telling me that I should see a therapist because I was always unhappy.

"You need to find out what's wrong with you."

He'd say, "You have a beautiful life, huge house, a husband that takes care of you, what could you possibly be unhappy about?"

My mind would shout the things I wanted to say, but my voice would not work. "It's you! It's you that makes me unhappy. You belittle me every step of the way, and you don't support me in any way."

I felt alone, questioning why we had gotten pregnant anyway, almost regretting that this baby would be coming into the world we'd made. I already had one son with special needs to take care of; how would I take care of two?

I was only unhappy when he was around. He made me feel on edge, not knowing what mood he was in or what he'd expect of me. My body was tense, my mind constantly questioning what was happening. We were two completely separate people still pretending life was normal.

I decided I would try therapy, that maybe there was something else causing my general unhappiness. This was a new experience for me, and I had never been to any sort of therapy before, so I was nervous and didn't know what to expect. My first session was an hour-long, and half of that was spent on paperwork and background info.

Where did you grow up? What is your career? Your family situation? All of it was very superficial and I felt almost silly being there. While I gave thorough answers to all of her questions, I didn't mention anything to do with my husband. I wasn't in therapy because of my husband's actions, I was in therapy because I was unhappy with my life. At least that's how he had instilled it in me.

I told her that I just felt a sense of overall sadness, that I didn't ever feel joyful, happy, surprised, or even angry. I mostly felt numb, just going through the everyday motions. I didn't cry in my session, but she passed me the box of tissues in case I started to. Near the end of our hour together, she suggested I try writing in a gratitude journal. She told me to try to find seven to ten things every day that made me feel grateful, no matter how big or small. Deep down, I hated this idea.

"But I don't *feel* ungrateful!" my soul wanted to yell, but that part of me stayed silent.

I thought, "I love being a mom, and I'm so excited to be having another baby. I love the beautiful summer weather and finally getting so much time outdoors."

These were things I believed to be true, things I knew I should be able to use to prove that I was not unhappy. But those things didn't make up for my inability to feel any sort of emotion. They weren't enough to bring me out of my funk, and I needed to find my real voice and bring her with me next time.

When I got home from my visit with the therapist, Scott was waiting for me in the kitchen with a giant smile. "How did it go? What did you talk about?"

My body instantly became stiff, annoyed that he even asked. "Not much, just about how I've been feeling."

"And how *is* it that you've been feeling? What did you tell her?" He asked, with so much attitude that I started to realize he wasn't going to back down.

I quickly became protective of myself, not understanding why he was pressing me for so much detail. Trying to find a way to give him some information without the intimate details of my time with the therapist, I simply replied, "We just talked about what my day looks like and tried to come up with ways to try to feel better."

"Well, did you talk about me? I don't get it, you just talked about your *day*? Did you tell her that you have a perfect life and there's no reason you shouldn't be happy? Did she bring up anti-depressants or anything?" He was getting upset now. He wanted me to be fixed, he wanted me to have one therapy session and come out with a plan to be better. And he wanted to make sure I wasn't blaming him for my unhappiness.

"We decided that I would start a gratitude journal so that I could start writing down things that I'm grateful for during the day." I had to give him something, something concrete so he would know I was trying.

He started laughing, "Well, you should have plenty to write in there every day!" then gave up and walked away.

The first few days of journaling went ok, and I did find that it was fairly easy to come up with the suggested number of things I was grateful for. "Joey scooped out the rest of the hummus dish with a cracker today! He is such a great eater."

"It's kind of fun doing laundry now that we have this new, cobalt blue washer and matching dryer."

"That butterfly has really beautiful, purple wings!"

I started to like looking for the beauty in the little things. I actively started paying attention to every detail, excited that I found more and more things to put in my journal. I would often put down ten for the day and then start adding more for the next day just in case I couldn't find enough tomorrow. Scott would occasionally ask me about it, joking "What did you find to make you happy today?"

There wasn't a single part of me that wanted to share my notes, my secrets; he would just make fun of me for finding joy in such little things. One of the days had resulted in me getting a call from the school district's bus company to say that they had found transportation from Joey's daycare to preschool. This had been causing me a lot of stress in the previous week or so because I didn't know how I was going to get him from point A to B and back again. This news had me nearly over-the-top excited. I was so thankful to have had a solution just drop into my lap. I told Scott about this, saying "I got the best news today!" and proceeded to tell him about the bussing situation.

"That's what you consider the best news? I expected you to say you won the lottery or something! Give me a break." This was exactly the reason I hadn't wanted to share any of my journal entries with him and never did again.

Our fifth wedding anniversary transpired one month before our second child was born. Scott had been traveling a lot for work, going to "Michigan" or "Chicago", sometimes "Iowa." The truth is, I had no idea where he was going. His job shouldn't have required any travel at all, but he was always coming up with an excuse for needing to visit these places. I learned not to question him on it because I wouldn't get the truth anyway. I also knew that I didn't have a plan for what to do if I found out he'd been lying.

I decided I wanted to do something special to celebrate our anniversary, just the two of us. Five years seemed like a pretty decent milestone, one that was worthy of celebration, and I had been feeling incredibly disconnected from him. He rarely checked in while he was gone, and he always seemed preoccupied when he was at home.

Being nearly ready to give birth, our options for what to do were pretty limited to somewhere local and low-key. So, I booked us a hotel room that overlooked the cathedral where we had gotten married five years before. I planned to have a romantic dinner followed by anniversary sex and the chance to sleep in for probably one of the last times before the baby came.

Normally when traveling, he would drive himself to the airport and park in the lot there. This time, however, he had taken a car service and I said that I would pick him up because I had something planned. He obliged, and even though I could tell he was a little irritated, he allowed me to collect him from the airport. His flight landed around 5 pm and as soon as he got in the car, I could tell he was exhausted, but I was excited and cheerful and wasn't going to let him bring me down too.

Ready to let him in on my surprise, I said excitedly, "I got a sitter for Joey and booked us a room at the St Paul Hotel for the night!"

I looked over at him with a giant smile on my face looking for his reaction.

"Oh, ok. I was looking forward to just going home and resting." He replied, wearily, not even looking up at me.

The smile slowly dropped from my cheeks. I know that traveling can take it out of a person, but I couldn't understand why he was so tired, and why he seemingly wasn't interested in spending time with me.

"Ok," I said, "Well, I guess you could take a little nap, and then we can go to dinner," hoping to still make this a successful date night.

The hotel was only about twenty minutes away from the airport, so we got there quickly and brought our bags up to the room to get settled in. Since he hadn't expected the extra night away, I packed him some additional clothes in my bag. As soon as we got into the room, he fell face down onto the bed and closed his eyes. Defeated, I walked over to the window to check out the view. It was incredible! Our window was filled with the image of the massive church perched on the hill on the horizon. I smiled again, excited to be getting a night away with my husband, and I looked over at him to ask him to come and see, but he was half asleep and obviously completely uninterested. My excitement faded, wondering if he would just remain there for the rest of the evening.

I decided I'd let him rest for a bit, hoping that would help him be in the mood to be here with me. I sat down in the oversized armchair in the corner of the room. It had a big enough ottoman to make it a comfortable second bed. I pulled out my phone to browse social media and pass the time. After about thirty minutes he started to stir, opening his eyes to see me sitting across the room.

"Ugh, sorry," he said, "I guess I was just really tired." and laughed at himself.

Trying to be understanding, I replied, "I guess. It's alright, I figured you just needed a quick nap."

Scott slowly got up from the bed, rubbing his eyes and fixing his hair before grabbing for his suitcase. He pulled out a giant shopping bag, stark white with bold black lettering on the front that said, "PRADA."

"I brought you something for our anniversary," he said, trying to sound excited.

I took the bag from him, unsure what to expect inside. I'd never dreamed of owning anything from Prada. I slowly untied the black ribbon that held the two handles together and reached inside to discover the contents. It was a designer bag of some sort, but I couldn't quite tell what its use was; it was so big. I looked at his face, hoping for some connection, some glimpse into his thoughts. He was smiling and said, "It's a diaper bag!" with enough excitement for both of us.

"Ohhhh!" I said, pulling the gift from the bag to examine it. It was absolutely beautiful. The outside was a shiny, navy nylon that almost looked black. It had gold metal accents, including the Prada logo on the front. There were pockets galore inside, all the perfect sizes for diapers, bottles, blankets, and all other things "baby."

"Thank you!" I gushed while I went over to hug him. As I put my arms around him, for the first time since I'd seen him that day, he swung one arm around my shoulders and patted me lightly on the back the way you might hug your grandma. He pulled away and announced that he was going to take a shower so that we could go down for dinner.

"Ok! I'll just be here admiring my new bag," I responded cheer-fully, trying to keep the mood light for both of us.

As I sat on the bed with the bag on my lap, I tried to be happy about the bag. It was a girl's dream – a fancy designer bag of any kind - and here I was with a designer diaper bag of all things. The only higher-end purse I'd ever owned was a pink velvet Juicy Couture purse I had bought myself when I hit a $1,000 jackpot at the casino on my birthday several years before.

Since then, I had a few knock-off purses, vowing I would never pay that much for just a purse again. Girls would say, "I love your purse!" as in, "Is that a real Prada?" At least with the fake Prada purse, I could say, "It's a fake!" and we'd laugh like girls do when they say they got an amazing deal on something they're wearing. But this was a real Prada, and I felt the same about this diaper bag as I did about the brand-new BMW SUV he had bought me – I felt like a fraud, like I was trying to be rich when I wasn't.

With this bag, I wouldn't be able to laugh with them about it. I would have to just say thank you to their admiration, and that would make me feel like a snob because I wasn't like them anymore, joking about the knock-off purses we had. I didn't feel rich. I didn't have any real money to my name. But my husband liked to spend money on these fancy things, just not on what I considered the necessities, like a savings account, or the mortgage. He lived in the now, and as long as he could spend money now, that's what mattered.

It's not that I wasn't grateful or excited about the bag; the feelings were so much more than that. He made me feel like he was the only one that mattered; that he made the money, and he should choose how we spent it.

It was that he hadn't shown a morsel of interest in me since I'd seen him that day, essentially tossing an expensive gift at me as a replacement for an emotional connection. I knew that this designer bag was bought as an after-thought at the airport on his way home, and that made me feel unimportant and alone.

A week went by and I met with my therapist again, discussing my journal as planned. She was surprised that I found it so easy to come up with things to be grateful for, and we chatted through my notes. "How did this exercise make you feel?" she asked.

"Pretty good." I started, "I liked being able to stop and smell the roses."

This time, I gained some courage to bring up some of my feelings about Scott. Almost embarrassed, I said, "I feel like I'm struggling to find much joy with my husband. He's been distant the past couple months, traveling a lot for work and just not engaging at home."

She looked at me, intrigued, probably wondering why I hadn't mentioned this the first time we met. Nudging me to go on, I continued, "Sometimes he'll come up behind me to give me a hug, try to kiss my neck, and my body recoils away from him."

"Why do you think that is?" she asked. "How does he react when you do that?"

"I don't like him being close to me, it makes me feel uncomfortable and I react impulsively. But then I feel bad, and I know it upsets him, so I quickly try to play it off, hugging him from the front instead."

"Hmmm, this sounds like something we should dig into in our next session." We were nearly out of time, and the last bit of info I gave her was a pretty big indicator that I had some work to do in therapy. She wrapped up our session by asking me to continue with my gratitude journal, but to also make note of when I physically react or feel not connected to my husband. Not surprisingly, it was this task that I felt most intimidated by. I hadn't paid much attention to how he made me feel, or when. Mentioning this one thing to her made it real and a noticeable problem in my marriage. Now I was to actively look for these signs and write them down, and I had to make extra sure he wasn't going to come across my notes.

The week that followed was especially bad between the two of us. He was irritated with every little thing that Joey did, twice kicking him in the butt just enough for him to lose his balance and tip over, ending in tears for both of them. One of those times Joey did a faceplant into the bed and came up with a bloody nose. "I'm so, so sorry!" Scott said although I'm not sure if he was apologizing to me, Joey, or himself. I scooped Joey up, hugging him tightly, removing him from being in the same room as Scott.

I didn't know what to do anymore, I didn't know how to behave with him around. Everything upset him and being around him made me anxious and irritable. Yet, nothing changed. I continued with the status quo, trying to avoid as much interaction or altercation as I could. To try to please Scott, I agreed we could start going out with other couples on the weekends, as he had requested. On the way downtown to meet some friends for dinner, we passed a daycare center that had just been built along one of the roads I took to work. I remarked out loud, mostly to myself, "Oh, I didn't know they put a Goddard school there."

Scott replied with disgust, "Ugh, we're going out tonight and all you have to talk about is a daycare? Can't you just be my wife tonight and not a mom?"

I was silenced and didn't bring up a conversation for the rest of the night, politely engaging in the discussions that seemed to be normal for the rest of the group. Clearly, I didn't know what should and shouldn't be discussed on date night.

The date night was Thursday, and I was scheduled to go back to see my therapist on Tuesday. But I didn't go, and I never went back to meet with her again. Because in between Thursday and Tuesday was Father's Day and the day I found out that Scott had been having an affair for at least the last six months, nearly my entire pregnancy. I didn't go back because I now had a reason for why he'd been so distant, so terrible at home. I knew the reason for my unhappiness and no reason to "get better" just for him. I was angry and saw going to therapy as something I was doing because *he* wanted me to be fixed, and I was no longer in the mood to play along. I ghosted my therapist without ever giving her the closure that I finally had my answer. I felt vindicated, that it hadn't been me with the problem, even if I had no idea how I would move forward.

The Narcissist

Narcissistic personality disorder (NPD) is a mental disorder in which people have an inflated sense of their own importance, a deep need for admiration, and a lack of empathy for others. But behind this mask of ultra-confidence lies a fragile self-esteem that's vulnerable to the slightest criticism. - Mayo Clinic.

The term "narcissist" comes from the Greek myth of Narcissus, in which a dude falls in love with his own reflection in a pool of water. However, that is not the dude I'm going to be talking about. The guy in my story is one that I spent all of my 20s with; a man I grew to love, marry and have children with. But when you're married to someone to whom image is everything, you don't talk about the bad stuff; you don't want to let people see your problems.

When Scott and I were first dating, he insisted I was a "Jessica" and not a "Jess" or "Jessie." He would tell me that he didn't like the nickname, Jess, always introducing me to others as *Jessica*, and correcting them if they called me Jess. I thought it was endearing having someone think I was poised enough to not go by a nick-name, and I didn't mind using my formal name.

Towards the end of our relationship, Scott would say my name, _Jessica_, with such disdain and contempt that I began to cringe at the sound of my own name. He'd enunciate each sound so that you could see the "Je" slithering through his teeth, hear the hiss of the "ss", the short "i" dripping with ick, and finally, spitting the "ca" at me. Every time he said it like that I cowered inside like a small child in trouble, yet the woman in me would fill with irri-tation and ire, wanting to shout, "don't _call_ me that!" But I couldn't tell him not to call me that, because then he would know it both-ered me and he would use that to have power over me. Turns out, he knew that without me having to say it; it's _why_ he did it. Scott used something so simple as my name as a way to exert his control over me.

Image was everything to Scott, and "elite" people like him shouldn't have to cater to the emotional needs of the people around them. It's nearly impossible to get help for a true narcis-sist, or to even get them to recognize they have a problem because, in their own eyes, they are perfect; it is everyone else that is flawed and problematic. They have an excessive sense of self-importance, an extreme preoccupation with themselves, and lack empathy for others. They don't seem to _suffer_ at all, it's everyone around them that does, enduring the lies and manipulation.

One could say narcissists lack a "moral compass" and do not follow the traditional right and wrongs of the world. A relation-ship with a narcissist consists of deep, severe, and prolific mind games, a never-ending nightmare, an inescapable emotional roller-coaster. I felt completely mind f***ed by the person I thought loved me and found it incredibly difficult to explain the whys and hows of what I'd experienced.

"I know you more than you even know yourself" Scott would often say to me.

Even though my thoughts and feelings weren't how he

described them, I believed him. I thought it was a sweet gesture for him to show that he loved me by really "knowing" me.

I would see him lie to others all the time and would brush it off as his "salesman" personality and didn't consider these seemingly minor infractions to be malicious or harmful. What I didn't recognize or realize was that he was also lying to me, about everything.

I am so ashamed to talk about it now, ashamed for being naïve enough to not see that he was controlling my reality and telling me truths that he wanted me to believe. Husbands don't lie to their wives; they love their wives, and their bond is a special one based on trust, empathy, and honesty. I offered those things to Scott and he turned those qualities against me, altering my world into one he could manipulate and control.

A manipulative person will say something with absolute conviction, and over time the people around will begin to believe him. I began to doubt myself often with Scott, *He seems so sure, and he seems so smart... I could be wrong.*

In her book, *The Gaslight Effect: How to Spot and Survive the Hidden Manipulation Others Use to Control Your Life*, Robin Stern writes, "The Gaslight Effect results from a relationship between two people: a *gaslighter*, who needs to be right in order to preserve his own sense of self and his sense of having power in the world; and the *gaslightee*, who allows the gaslighter to define her sense of reality because she idealizes him and seeks his approval."

To read that description of the gaslightee, *"because she idealizes him and seeks his approval,"* makes me nauseous now because I know that to be true of myself at the beginning of our relationship. Having never had a real boyfriend and not having a close relationship with my dad, I clung to his special treatment and needed his approval. I loved that he told me he cared about me, I loved the sexual attention he gave me, the gifts and fancy lifestyle he provided me. What I didn't see was that these things were in response to me giving him what he needed to keep him happy, not because I was special to him. I learned very quickly to just go with the flow with him, not to question the hows and whys. If he was happy, I was happy, and I wanted him to be happy!

I had never heard the term Narcissistic Personality Disorder until I found support groups on Facebook during the early stages of our divorce, specifically, *One Mom's Battle* run by author and narcissistic abuse survivor, Tina Swithin. The more and more I read about it, the more it appeared to fit Scott's "personality" and my experiences with him. I sought out information, Googling everything I could find. I took psychology courses in college and knew that the DSM-5 was a manual used to assess and diagnose mental disorders. Curious, I looked up what it had to say about NPD.

The following are characteristics of NPD as described in the DSM-5 (Diagnostic and Statistical Manual of Mental Disorders).

A pervasive pattern of grandiosity (fantasy or behavior), need for admiration, and with lack of empathy, beginning by early adulthood, as indicated by at least five of the following:

- *Having an exaggerated sense of self-importance*
- *Expecting to be recognized as superior even without achievements that warrant it*
- *Exaggerating your achievements and talent*
- *Being preoccupied with fantasies about success, power, brilliance, beauty, or the perfect mate*
- *Believing that you are superior and can only be understood by or associate with equally special people*
- *Requiring constant admiration*
- *Having a sense of entitlement*
- *Expecting special favors and unquestioning compliance with your expectations*
- *Taking advantage of others to get what you want*
- *Having an inability or unwillingness to recognize the needs and feelings of others*

- *Being envious of others and believing others envy you*
- *Behaving in an arrogant or haughty manner*

Scott had them all. He was a master at emotional blackmail, using fear, obligation, and guilt (FOG) to control me. To not upset him and avoid a tantrum, I would do what I could just to keep him satisfied, putting my own needs aside. I felt obligated to take care of everything at home because he "worked so hard" to support our family, even though I also worked outside of the home. And the guilt factor was possibly the worst; a narcissist projects their insecurities onto others, which meant I was constantly having to defend seemingly normal actions.

The term "narcissist" gets thrown around a lot, usually when describing selfish people, and I think we all have someone in our lives that fits the criteria to some extent. I struggle with describing Scott that way because the use of the word is so pervasive in our culture that it feels like it somewhat diminishes the damage that can be done by a true narcissist. Being selfish and self-absorbed is not the same as abusing others to get what you want. Scott has never sought therapy or any sort of treatment because there's nothing wrong with him, in his eyes, of course. He can do no wrong, so it is not his fault if someone is upset by his actions.

"Don't be so sensitive."

"Take a joke!"

"You shouldn't have done XYZ and I wouldn't have had to..."

My experience lies within being married to, divorced from, and co-parenting with a malignant narcissist.

When I laid out all the ways Scott had been lying to me, he said I should've been a private eye. The lies became so normal, so every day, they didn't even *feel* like lies anymore. Rather, they were just his personality.

The simplest things would be exaggerated and inflated. When I was pregnant with Joey, we were selling his motorcycle; something that he had bought from eBay on a whim, almost by accident when his lowball bid won. A couple came to look at the motorcycle and when they asked why we were selling it, he told them we were expecting twins and didn't need the motorcycle anymore.

Now, I was standing right next to him, clearly a few months along. Wouldn't mentioning I was pregnant have been sufficient? Why had he needed to tell them it was twins? "Go big or don't go at all" was part of his psyche. I stood next to my husband, going along with his falsehoods just because I wasn't going to call out my husband in front of strangers. I didn't want to make public situations awkward and uncomfortable. Instead, I would confront him about it afterward, asking him why he said it was twins.

"Who cares?" was always his response.

How about me? *I* care; I cared that he couldn't be honest in even the most straightforward situations. We were having a baby and no longer wanted to have the motorcycle. Why do we need to be having *two* babies for it to make sense? The lies felt like madness.

In college, I went to London for a week for a class credit in clothing design. *One week* was how long I was there. Years later I ran into someone Scott had worked with and she asked me how my time studying in Europe was. I was a little confused because I never "studied in Europe." To me, that sounded like something fancy people do.

She repeated, a little differently this time, "Scott said you were studying in Europe for a semester in college." That's when I understood he had told her I went away to Europe for school and that we had broken up while I was gone, so it was okay that he was seeing other girls.

I responded, unable to contain my laugh, "Oh! Nope, that never happened. I went to London for a week for a class, but that was it. It was a lovely trip, though."

She let out a laugh as well and rolled her eyes, saying, "Ugh! He is such a liar!"

We remodeled our bedroom after he had taken several trips to Vegas and became bored with our suburban lifestyle. He wanted flashy and new, in so many more ways than one; if only I'd understood then that this desire for "better" included me. He hoped that by improving the world around him, life at home would be more tolerable.

Life doesn't work in such simple terms, and the grass is rarely greener on the other side. Before we began the remodel, he asked me to work with our friend Dana, who is an interior designer. She took me around to the interior design showrooms to pick out fabrics and colors and develop a theme for the room. We spent hours walking around the marketplace, gathering samples and fabric swatches for the drapes, wallpaper, bedding, flooring, etc.

This process took several hours and a lot of our friend's time and resources. However, once we started talking prices, Scott was appalled, and couldn't believe these things could cost so much, demanding I tell her we wouldn't be moving forward. I was embarrassed and felt so horrible for all of the time she had invested in this. I sat in our room and sobbed. How was I going to tell her, "Sorry for wasting your time, but we don't need your services anymore as they are too expensive."

I had no idea what our budget was and since his plans were so grandiose, I only assumed he knew what we were going to be spending. That's the thing, he wouldn't talk with me about our finances or budget. I felt naïve, even now, for just doing whatever he wanted me to do. I didn't know how much money he brought home, only that he didn't have a salary because he earned straight commission.

I didn't know how much our mortgage payment was because he bought the home before we were married, and it was in his name only. I had no idea what our monthly expenses were or how much the cars cost. He simply took care of it all and I never asked, as I knew it wasn't something he wanted to discuss. He didn't want people, especially me, to know he'd rob Peter to pay Paul. He wanted to be left alone to buy and do the things he needed to feel wealthy.

Even though he would tell me over and over that I wasn't good with finances, or that I couldn't maintain a budget, he did it in a way that made it feel like he was taking care of me. He would joke about it, saying things like, "Awwww, did you make sure to make your Macy's payment this month?" or "Just write a check from the business account for that doctor bill."

These were simple things to pay, and he wanted me to feel like I shouldn't have a care about money at all, that the only thing I needed to worry about was making sure I paid for my wardrobe that month. I guess I liked that I didn't have to think about the house or car payments, but I didn't understand how sick and one-sided our relationship was.

After we decided not to move forward with the interior designer, I still had to find a way to fulfill his dream of a Vegas-worthy bedroom. I went to a local paint supply store and found a wallpaper that we both liked, but the cost was still way too high for our budget, which I found out was basically nothing. I consider myself frugal and figured I'd see what I could find online instead. I ended up finding the same wallpaper somewhere else for about half the cost. I was so excited, both for my frugality and because we'd be able to get the wallpaper I had fallen in love with.

It was a textured fabric with teeny-tiny waves in just the perfect shade of amethyst; certainly, a party-in-the-bedroom design. We hired someone to hang it (because Scott said we couldn't be bothered to do such "peasant work"), and it was perfect. It went flawlessly with the new designer carpet and the mounted TV with color-changing LED mood lights behind it.

Once it was finished, we had his parents over to see the remodel. Scott's dad, John, is working-class, a frugal man, refusing to buy something new when he could fix it up, "good as new" himself. However, he is one of those unassumingly wealthy men, a millionaire that has only recently reached the point where he feels comfortable spending the money he has cultivated over the years. Scott's mom, Lucy, is an adorably fashionable sweetheart that stands barely over five feet tall, always in sparkles and heels. Lucy was a stay-at-home mom who adored her children, and as they got older, she started selling makeup to the ladies in town for some extra spending money. Lucy loves with all her heart and could not possibly have a single enemy.

Throughout our years together, we saw his parents frequently, nearly every Sunday, and we all enjoyed each other's company. Excited to show off our remodel, the four of us were standing in our newly decked-out bedroom, amongst the smell of fresh carpet and wallpaper adhesive. Scott said to his parents, "Don't you just love the wallpaper? Jessica was able to special order it from France and it took about eight weeks to get here. It was really expensive, but we loved it, so who cares?"

John and Lucy just nodded their heads and politely told us, "Yes, we love it!"

Yet there was a hint of them saying it just to please Scott, or maybe us collectively. Maybe it was that they didn't really like it because it was too trendy for their taste, or maybe they thought we'd needlessly spent money on something so impractical as imported wallpaper.

It was also possible that my senses were heightened because I just heard my husband tell a flat-out lie to his parents. His dad is wise with money and would have been more than thrilled to hear that we got it online for half the price it would have been in the store.

I stood there and listened to him go on and on about how great it was, wanting to scream "that's not at all how it went!" but feeling powerless and incapable of calling out my husband's lies.

This same scenario happened over and over through the years. Scott would tell some lie and I'd be faced with either calling him out on the lie or simply nodding in agreement. I made a point to never *agree* with the story he told, but rather to simply not disagree. If I just nodded or shrugged my shoulders, it was still just his lie, not my own. There were two sides to nearly every story. The real one, and the one he told. Over time, those stories became harder and harder to keep straight. Sometimes, I forgot which was the lie, especially true of those that were told often.

Emotional abuse and manipulation can be hard to recognize and are often brushed off as just a personality trait. Scott was just a funny guy, liked to make people laugh. He was opinionated and liked to make his opinions known. But I didn't realize that an opinion is someone's point of view, not to be taken as a demand to do something just because of their opinion. Being funny shouldn't be at the expense of others or it becomes bullying.

Me? A victim of abuse?? That's laughable! And I almost believe it myself, because I was trained to believe that it was a joking matter, that it was just for fun and I was too stuffy.

Like vs Need

"You're going to be happy," said Life, "but first, I'm going to make you strong." - *Anonymous*

Father's Day, 2012 was the definitive beginning of the end of our marriage. The day before, Scott's younger cousin got married and Scott was a groomsman, while Joey was a ringbearer. I have one picture of the two of us with Joey from that day. The three of us stood holding hands, Joey in the middle, in front of the altar of the Catholic church. I was three weeks away from my due date with our second, wearing a knee-length flowy green dress and heels. I had borrowed the dress from a coworker who had recently had a baby because I didn't want to spend the money to buy a maternity dress for this one occasion. The two boys were dressed in their dapper black suits with peach-colored bow ties. We looked like a smiley, happy family, waiting to welcome a new little one into our clan. However, getting this happy picture taken was about the only time I saw Scott that day. He kept himself out of sight, celebrating with the wedding party who were all about ten years younger than him. He was drunk all day, and I was swollen and tired from the warm June sunshine.

Even though Scott and Joey were in the wedding party together, I was in charge of everything Joey needed to do: wedding party photos, walking the ring down the aisle, waiting endlessly for dinner, etc. Scott never checked in on us and wanted me to keep our son out of his hair, completely ignoring us all day. He didn't eat dinner with us, he didn't do any dancing with us; he didn't even acknowledge the fact that we existed. The weird thing was this was a wedding on *his* side of the family. Even still, he showed no shame in leaving us alone the entire day. Joey and I sat with Scott's parents during the dinner, while he sat at the head table. We sat with his parents while he was out on the dance floor with the bridesmaids. I only now realize how odd it was that no one seemed to notice I was left to myself all day long. After dinner and a few songs on the dance floor, he dismissed us officially and sent me home with Joey. I didn't hear from him again until he came home at noon the following day – which happened to be Father's Day.

When he finally showed up at home, he was completely hungover, seemingly pleased with himself for having a good time. Joey and I were playing outside when he arrived, and I ran inside to grab the watermelon I had cut up earlier so that the three of us could sit on the front porch, eating watermelon together, keeping my mouth otherwise occupied so I wouldn't yell at him in front of Joey. He was trying to be cheerful for Joey's sake and to not let on just how hungover he was. I was livid with him and could hardly contain my soul-deep desire to scream at him for abandoning us the entire day prior, for not coming home until noon on Father's Day, for not caring one bit about anyone but himself. But I kept myself together long enough to put Joey down for a nap.

When I came back outside, he was still sitting in the same chair I'd left him in thirty minutes before. He welcomed me back by saying "We need to work on our relationship."

I could only muster in reply, "Ya think? What the hell is going on?"

Easing my swollen belly into the deep wooden Adirondack chair outside next to his, I laid into him exactly how I felt about his behavior lately and how little he cared about me or our children. We were due to have another child in three weeks, and here we were having to have a conversation about our relationship needing work. This baby was not conceived in hopes of saving our marriage or offering a new beginning for us. This baby was a choice we made to add to our family, even if unplanned, to grow in love together, and it was like he hadn't even noticed it had been present in our lives for the past nine months.

My ranting did nothing but make him tune me out further. He requested me to go get us notebooks and pens because he wanted us to individually write down the things we'd "like to have," and those we "need to have," for our marriage to be happy again. I felt like I had left my body at this point. I couldn't quite understand what he was asking. I shouted in my head, "Isn't it obvious? I need you to be my partner and to show that you care about me and my feelings. I need you to pull your weight around here and to *love* me!"

I thought I was a fairly reasonable person and that I hadn't demanded too much from my husband, but I truly didn't know anymore, so I decided to go along with the ask. We'd never actually had a conversation like this before, expressing our desires and dissatisfactions, so part of me thought this was a great suggestion.

However, I didn't feel like I could be honest with him without getting made fun of. He had always made fun of other people for being "too emotional" or "sensitive." My hands were sweating, and my vision began to blur. I choked back my tears because I was NOT going to let him see me cry. What the hell would I write? What was the difference between what I would like and what I would need? Aren't they the same? What happens if I say I *need* something, but he doesn't agree? I can't be too indulgent, and I'm not able to be vulnerable enough to tell him my deepest wants and needs. I have spent the past nine months preparing to bring a new life into our world, and in the blink of an eye, I'm being asked what I *need* to save our marriage. *Do I want to? I don't even like being around you! Wouldn't life be better if you would just go?* But I can't say any of that; I am not able to be hurtful like you.

I started at the top of the page with two columns; the one on the left said, "Things I'd like," and the column on the right said, "Things I need." I could not get my brain to focus. How long did I have? How many should I write? Not too many, but also enough to look like I cared. I glanced at him without him noticing, and found him scribbling away, clearly having none of the inner turmoil I was. I started with the "Things I'd like" column because it felt safer, less needy.

I wrote, "I'd *like* to be able to sleep in a little bit one morning a week." This felt reasonable. I put our son to bed every single night and I woke up with him before dawn every single day. I was also starting to get very tired at the end of my pregnancy. It felt like a small ask, "to rest for a little bit while you take care of our son," but I had to put a parameter around it so he knew it was just once a week, and only for a little bit in the morning.

"I'd *like* you to be home by 6 pm most nights of the week." For the past six months, he'd been coming home after Joey was asleep so that he didn't have to deal with him. I wanted to be able to have dinner together and enjoy some family time before bed.

I wrote, "I'd *like* to start going to church as a family once a month." I put this one specifically for him because he used to enjoy going to church before we were married, and I thought it might help him focus his attention back on his family. I struggled with what else to put down, and for the life of me, I cannot remember anything that I put in the "I *need*" column. I can't imagine I put anything there, because I honestly didn't see myself deserving of anything enough to consider it a need in this conversation.

After I just couldn't write down another thing without feeling immense embarrassment and doubt, I asked, "Are you ready?"

He replied with a laugh, "Been ready. And I can't wait to hear what you wrote!"

Of course, the "I can't *wait*" was dripping with sarcasm, implying that he already knew he wasn't interested in what I had to say. We went through my list first, and to my surprise, he balked at almost every single one of them. Should I have been surprised? No, but therein lies the biggest problem: I was continuously surprised by his behavior, which made it easier to forgive every time. Everything was a joke with him and I became great at eye-rolling his comments away. He would laugh about it and then hug me as if to apologize for being a jerk.

He thought it was way too much for me to ask to sleep in because he was not going to get up at the crack of dawn or before (literally) with Joey. He just wasn't going to do it, not even once a week, and made it very clear he wouldn't. He scoffed that I requested he be home by 6 pm but said that he would try. This was his one give, that he would try to be home for dinner most nights. It became so normal to me that he made the rules in our house; that he got to do whatever it was that he wanted, and I was to be waiting for him, whenever and wherever he wanted me.

Once we ran out of things to go over from my list, which wasn't finished because I became too angry and embarrassed to continue, we went on to his list. His requests were not at all what I expected them to be. I don't know how I could've prepared for something like this, to anticipate what was making my husband unhappy in our marriage. I would have expected the mention of more sex, or to suggest I see a therapist to try and not be so angry all the time, but I could not have even begun to guess what he would actually say. The first item on his list of things he'd like to improve our marriage was, "I'd *like* you to dress sexier."

I went to college to study retail and fashion and had always considered myself somewhat fashionable with a nod toward classic sense of style. Sure, I could skank it up a bit on a trip to Vegas, but that wasn't going to be my everyday attire. Nor *should* it be for a pregnant woman in her thirties. He completely ignored the fact that the reason I had gained thirty pounds and a giant belly was that I was *pregnant,* and my style had changed because I had been wearing maternity clothes for the past few months. Pregnant women are often told they are beautiful and glowing, and from what I hear, can even be considered *sexy* to their part-ners. My "chubby" (aka *p r e g n a n t*) body was a turn-off for him, and he wanted me to fix it.

The second item on his list was, "I'd *like* us to get more babysitters and go out with other couples every weekend." Every weekend? We already had several babysitters a month, and thank-fully the three sisters across the street were almost always avail-able if we wanted to make plans. But this wasn't even a request for more date nights, this was a request to go out and party with *other* couples *every* weekend. This was a request saying, "I hate my life with you, and I want to fill it with other people as much as possi-ble." I had no words, nothing to say in response. These things were so superficial and not about our relationship in the least. I felt defeated and deflated and speechless. He didn't care. He main-tained his arrogant attitude and kept going through his list.

The real winner was one straight out of a porno, and he'd saved it for last because he seemed to think it was the most important. With a completely sincere and even tone, he said, "I'd *like* you to give another man a blowjob while I watch, within the next three months." He'd said it about as casually as you'd call your mom and ask her to come over to dinner. No pretense, no emotion. These were supposed to be the things he wanted to make our *marriage* better. I felt sick, trying to hold back the vomit and tears, feeling ridiculous for entertaining this idea at all. I didn't know what to think or feel or *do*. I sat there not knowing what to say.

I tried to tell him that his desires for our marriage were not something I could take seriously, and he returned the sentiment towards my list. We were essentially at a standstill, upset with the other for the vast difference in our desired improvements in our marriage. We eventually got up and went our separate ways, him to go sleep off his hangover and me to go take care of our son who had woken from his nap.

Bubble Bath

I am not sure how we managed to get through the rest of the day together, but I know we pretty much stayed out of each other's way. After I made dinner and cleaned up, I went to put Joey to bed. Scott decided he needed to relax and take a bath; likely still hungover from the hard day of partying the day before. Him, a bath? Weird. But I guess it was *Father's Day* so I suppose he could do whatever he wanted. I knew something had been going on for a while, weeks if not months. He was spending less and less time at home and he'd been getting a lot of text messages, keeping his phone locked and near him at all times. Even though this newish routine didn't go unnoticed, I never said anything; I never asked what he was up to or what he was hiding. I guess I knew deep down that he would never tell me the truth anyway, so it wasn't worth asking.

He'd get this grin on his face that he tried to hide while reading his texts, and it was just clear that something was going on. It irritated me to my core, that I wasn't a part of this secret, that he *had* a secret. This fueled my impatience and anger toward him. I only occasionally gave a quick "What's so funny?" or "Who are you talking to?", only to be met with a "nothing" or "no one" in response.

We were standing in the kitchen, with nothing to say, when he finally mumbled, "I'm going to take a bath." I watched him set his phone down on the counter across the kitchen from where I was standing. It was lit up and not locked. I knew from watching him and his phone routine that there was about a 10-15 second delay before the phone would lock from inactivity. For some reason, this particular time he had left his phone in the kitchen while he went to draw the bath. I watched him walk down the hall toward our bedroom and once I saw him turn the corner and out of sight, I darted across the room to tap on the screen to keep it alive. My stomach dropped at the extreme range of emotions running through me. I was panicked by the thought of getting caught, yet ecstatic at the opportunity to see just what was going on.

I started to sweat, tapping the screen every five seconds or so, to ensure it wouldn't lock. I thought I was going to throw up. I'd tap the screen, then walk away from the phone back to where I had been standing, just in case he came back out to get the phone. I was pacing the kitchen floor, anxiety filling every nerve in my body. This was a one-time opportunity for me to see the contents of his phone, and I was terrified of what I would find and what would happen to me if he found me looking. Why? *Why* had he left his phone? Was this a trap? Did he want me to look?

I heard the jets turn on in the tub and knew he was in the bath and therefore not coming back out for his phone. I picked up the phone and started looking through texts. He had been smart and deleted them frequently, but there was one message exchange still on the chain. It was just a phone number, no contact name stored. The number was not local, so I Googled the area code from my phone, and it was from Las Vegas. He'd been frequenting Vegas over the past several months, so that fact did not surprise me. There was only one message from this number and one message from him back.

The random number said, "I love you and miss you."

He replied, "I love you and miss you too. I'm going to bed, night!"

This exchange happened only minutes ago, while I was standing next to him in the kitchen. Even though I knew something had to be going on, seeing it made me sick. I became hot and instantly sweaty; rage filled within me and I could not believe this was happening. But I did know; somewhere buried inside, I knew. I walked straight into the bathroom where he was soaking in the jetted jacuzzi, anger and hatred across my face. He looked up at me, shocked that I was upset about something, and also irritated that I had come barging in. As calmly as I could, I asked, "Who's Vegas?"

He gazed at me, not with fear of getting caught with something, but almost with amusement that I had found out. "What are you talking about?" he asked, wryly.

"The text message to the Vegas number, that you love them and are going to bed," I replied with a snarl. "You left your phone unlocked on the counter and I went through it."

I couldn't bear to have this conversation with him sitting in the bathtub, me standing over him and talking over the hum of the jets, so I turned around and stormed out. With tears streaming down my face and my stomach flipped upside down, I waited back in the kitchen for him to come to talk to me.

He took his time getting out of the bath and joining me. I imagine it was more out of spite that he was now forced to talk about this, rather than fear of the conversation itself. The first thing he did was walk over to me, wrap his arms around me and say, "We will wait until the baby is born before discussing this."

I pushed him off of me and stared at him, my mouth hanging wide open. What was that supposed to mean? He thought that we would just go on about our lives as if nothing happened until the baby came? In what world would that be a possibility? He followed up with, "This is too upsetting for you to deal with the emotions right now. We will talk about it after the baby comes."

I wanted to know everything. I *had* to know everything. Who is she? Is *she* even a *she*? I only assumed this random number "I love you" would be a woman, but with no contact name given as a possible clue, I had no idea. How long had this been going on? How often did they talk, or see each other? He wouldn't give me anything, no details whatsoever, and tried to get me to stop talking about it altogether. I pushed him, yelled at him demanding, "How could you do this to me?" He enjoyed seeing me upset. There was no remorse from him, no attempt at an apology.

He said "I've been trying to tell you for a while that I'm not happy. I told you that you don't really turn me on anymore and that we don't have enough sex. What did you expect? Of *course* I went elsewhere; it's your fault this happened."

All I could think was, "What am I going to do?" My only thoughts at that moment were about how I was going to take care of our kids on my own. Where would we live? How do I bring this baby into this mess? I can't possibly ask friends or family to take us in. I have no one but this man standing in front of me, yet I want to get as far away from him as possible.

I said it out loud, "What am I going to do?" and that angered him.

He sneered back, "Why are you only thinking about yourself? Why aren't you trying to figure out how to make us better?" His adultery was my fault and my problem to fix.

Over the next few days, we managed to co-exist in the same house. There was a spare bedroom set up next to Joey's, and that's where I stayed. He would leave for work in the morning and return extremely late at night, and I tried to never see him. Days later, he decided to give me bits and pieces about what was going on, mostly because he wanted me to know the details to show off. Turned out that he'd been having an affair for several months with a female casino host in Vegas. She made him feel wanted and desired and that's exactly what he needed to feel. He told me that she was also unhappily married with a young child, but she wasn't ready to leave her husband yet. Is that the only reason he was still with me, because he had nowhere to go with her? Why was I still here?

The two of them were there for each other and found comfort in each other. He was so infatuated with her that he would text with her all day, talk to her on his drive home from work, and then have nothing left for me or Joey once he was home. He was bitter that he even had to come home to us and not to her, and he treated us with such disdain. He was never apologetic or sought forgiveness. He blamed his affair and infidelity on my "lack of love" for him and my inability to meet his needs. This is what people say, right? That their partner wasn't able to meet their needs and they found them met elsewhere. It's the *partner's* fault.

I truly don't know what more I could have done in our home and relationship that would have not resulted in him seeking admiration elsewhere. I worked forty hours a week, took care of our son's every need, kept a tidy house, and made dinner every night, while he yelled at me from the couch that I was too loud whilst doing the dishes. I did all the meal planning and grocery shopping, making sure to cater to whatever diet he was trying to follow. I cleaned up after dinner and did bath time, while he was nowhere in sight. I sometimes spent hours putting our three-and-a-half-year-old to bed. Joey still wanted to be bounced on the yoga ball, now

I did so with a basketball of a belly myself. I did all of the household cleaning and chores, except paying the bills because Scott didn't trust me with that.

If I asked him to help with things around the house he'd respond, "If it's too much work for you then hire someone to come in and do it."

He'd be gone, traveling every week, complaining that I just wasn't doing enough for him. He would complain that we weren't having enough sex, saying, "The only way I can feel a connection with you is by having sex with you." It was so hurtful every time he'd say it because he was telling me clearly, "I don't love *you*, I love having sex with you." But isn't it normal to need a connection with your partner to enjoy sex? I would try to have this conversation with him by retaliating, "Well, I need to feel loved and cared for by you to *want* to have sex with you."

I *hated* sex with him by then; even before I had found out about the affair, his emotional detachment and lack of any form of respect for me made it nearly impossible to tolerate his physical presence. It felt disgusting, and I avoided it at all costs. Sometimes, he'd come up behind me while I was doing the dishes and kiss my neck, asking if we could have sex later. My whole body would cringe, instinctively jolting away from his hot breath, not being able to stand being close to him a second longer.

My resentment toward him grew stronger every day. His reaction would be to say "I don't have any connection with you, and that makes me not want to help you around the house. If you're not attracted to me and won't have sex with me, then I just don't want to be around you."

"Good!" I thought, "I want you as far away from me as possible." But I couldn't say it. Even though he had said and done such awful things to me, I couldn't bring myself to say hurtful things back. I'd just let it go and hope things would magically get better on their own.

It's a Baby, Take Two

I don't recall too much of how the next three weeks went after that fateful Father's Day. I was avoiding my husband, working, and waiting for labor to begin while taking care of Joey. My due date was July 4, which was a Wednesday, and it came and went with no labor in sight. Finally, two days later on Friday night, my water broke while I was putting Joey to bed, though I wasn't sure that's what had happened at first. I was lying in bed with Joey, singing him to sleep. When he was finally asleep, I rolled my big belly to the side and sat up. It felt like I had peed my underwear, so I sat there for a minute, kind of in shock, but finally got up to go to the bathroom. It was a moment of "Holy crap, did I just pee my pants?" before I realized "Oh yea, what if that was my water that broke?" My water didn't break on its own with Joey, so I didn't know what it felt like and I wasn't expecting it.

After I went to the bathroom and realized it was a trickle that didn't stop, I determined it must be my water leaking. I was home alone with a toddler and Scott was out at the bar with friends, so I texted him to let him know I thought my water broke. He responded, "What do you mean you *think* your water broke? Did it or didn't it?" I told him that it had and that he needed to come home.

I called his dad and asked if he could come down to stay with Joey while we went to the hospital. Scott and his dad were both about thirty-five minutes away from our house, in different directions, and got to our house about the same time. By now, I was leaking a lot and was wearing a bath towel in my pants. I was starting to get nervous and in hindsight, it's a good thing that my labors are lengthy! It was about an hour after my water broke before we were on our way to the hospital, but I hadn't had any contractions yet, so there was no real rush to get there. Scott was quite buzzed from being out drinking at the bar, and he found the whole thing amusing. Given that we had hardly seen each other over the past couple of weeks, it felt incredibly odd to be driving to the hospital together to have this baby. We felt like strangers. He had pretended I wasn't pregnant for nearly the last nine months and was extremely blasé about the impending delivery.

Once we parked, we grabbed the bags and the big blue yoga ball that I was determined to bounce on until I pushed the baby out. He was embarrassed by the ball and insisted that I carry it while waddling with a bath towel stuffed in my pants to absorb the amniotic fluid that was running at a constant stream. We got admitted and set up camp in the labor and delivery room. I got dressed in the uber thin, open-back delivery gown and laid on the bed so they could confirm my water had broken. The nurse confirmed I was in labor and asked if I wanted some essential oils to create a soothing ambiance. "Sure! Lavender, please." I said, which was then dripped on a cotton ball housed inside of a small dixie cup. After a few inhales of the lavender-scented cotton ball, I sat on the blue yoga ball and began lightly bouncing in hopes of starting contractions. Scott was lying on the partner chair/bed next to my delivery bed, trying to get in a nap since not much was happening with me anyway. After ten minutes or so of bouncing in the lonely, darkened room, I was getting bored and realized I was freezing, so I decided that a hot shower sounded blissful.

I took off my hospital gown and was very thankful that Scott was asleep and wouldn't be able to see me naked. I felt so exposed and embarrassed standing there, so I rushed into the bathroom and closed the door. I turned on the shower and waited for it to get warm and steamy before stepping in and closing the curtain. It's an odd feeling being in a hospital bathroom. It is sort of like a small motel bathroom layout, with the toilet directly next to the sink and the shower across the room, but you're in a hospital, not on vacation. The shower is only a shower, and not a bathtub combo, which is a great thing for a not-so-nimble pregnant woman. I felt a little silly standing there in the shower, having absolutely no contractions or signs of labor, other than the leaky-faucet state of my vagina.

I was enjoying the heat of the shower water running over my shoulders and swollen tummy when, out of nowhere, contractions began at full force. My pain went from *zero* to almost unbearable instantly. I turned off the water, grabbed a towel, and climbed into bed just as a nurse came to check on me. I let her know what had happened and that my contractions had started. She let *me* know that the thermostat was broken, and the air conditioner was stuck in the on position. The room was stuck in the low sixties and I couldn't stop shivering. Scott was passed out in the chair next to me, leaving me to fend for myself. The nurses brought me an extra blanket from the warmer and were kind enough to oblige my foolish requests to get him a blanket and make sure he was comfortable too. They looked at him with eyes that said, "You're an asshole!" and then at me with sadness.

I couldn't stay on top of the contractions and was nearly in a state of panic because I was in so much pain. I was on all fours in the hospital bed, sobbing, with no one there to help me manage the pain. Scott was too annoyed with my cries and didn't know how to help, so he sat there and watched. The nurses ordered the epidural but there was a back-up, and it would be at least forty-five minutes until the anesthesiologist could be there. In the meantime, they had to get an I.V. started for fluids, but they couldn't find any suitable veins due to it being so fricken cold in the room, so they gave me hot packs for my hands to warm up.

Normally, my veins are big and blue and above the surface, a phlebotomist's dream! I was delirious, moaning "fuuuuuck" way more times than necessary from the pain. I tried to say it quietly, to keep my voice down, but I don't think I was as quiet as I thought I was. Scott kept shushing me, telling me to stop swearing and be quiet; my having our baby was an inconvenience and I was embarrassing him.

He tried lightly running his fingers along my upper arm, enough to make him feel like he was trying to help me, but it was only annoying me. Finally, just when I literally didn't know if I was going to be able to tolerate it much longer, they got the I.V. in and I was able to get the epidural. As soon as the anesthesiologist finished, I felt relief start to run in a wave from my belly down to my toes. A nurse came in with some contraption that had a blanket with a hairdryer-like attachment meant to send heat throughout quickly. That got me warm fast, and I wondered, "Where in the hell was this thing an hour ago?"

My labor lasted about another ten hours from the time I got the epidural. When it was time to push, the baby's heart rate would go down dangerously low, just as Joey's had done, so the nurse had me try pushing in different positions. I could feel that I was most effective at pushing when laying on my side, and the nurse agreed, but that was when it was bad for baby's heart rate. In the end, the doctor needed to use the vacuum to assist in delivery, just as he had when Joey was born.

With the final push, baby arrived with the telltale conehead from where the vacuum was suctioned to his head. They announced, "It's a boy!" and I was shocked because I was sure it was a girl this time. The entire pregnancy I had steered more toward girl things and girl names, most likely out of wishful thinking. They laid him on my chest, and I got to count all his fingers and toes and kiss his squishy cheeks. He was a pound heavier and an inch shorter than Joey, yet he seemed so tiny! It's amazing how quickly it all goes by.

Baby David and I laid in the delivery room together while we waited to be moved to the recovery room. He was a great nurser right from the start and we bonded instantly. I couldn't stop staring at his huge blue eyes, just like mine. Scott left almost immediately to go home and sleep it off, waiting just until we arrived at the recovery room before leaving. I felt relieved because I didn't have to entertain him anymore and I could spend time bonding with David in peace.

I remember after Joey was born, Scott did almost the same thing; he went home to sleep rather than stay with us in the hospital. When he finally came back to the hospital, he told me all about the porn he watched at home that made him feel so "relaxed and peaceful." Ugh, just what a new mother dreams to hear about, her husband going home to masturbate from the stress of his wife delivering their baby. I wish I would have been able to see his obsession with sex and porn earlier. Our entire relationship had been hyper-focused on sex, and when sex began to lack, he was done with me.

About two weeks after David was born, Scott didn't come home one night. We were still living together, but nothing had changed. I tried to sleep in our bed with Scott and he tried to act like he cared about us, at least for a while. I woke up around one in the morning to pump (David was a great sleeper from the start!) and I got a text from Scott saying that he was too drunk to drive and was staying at his friend's house. I responded immediately that it was unacceptable to not come home to your wife and brand-new baby, but never got a response back. I stood there in the kitchen, breast pump hooked up and milking away, staring at my phone, willing him to respond.

"What makes you think you can just do whatever you want, whenever you want?" I seethed at him in my head.

"Why do you not care about us? How can you just leave us home alone all the time? Don't you want to *see* your baby?" But I said nothing more, just unhooked the boob contraption and went back to bed.

Around 9 am the next morning, after still no word from Scott, I texted the friend that he said he was staying with.

"What is going on with Scott?" I asked, assuming that they must've talked about what's going on at home after a night of drinking. "How does he think it's ok to just not come home?"

This friend was a groomsman in our wedding; he had stayed with us for a couple of months while he found a new place to live after he and his wife separated. We were supposed to take care of each other! But he didn't respond to my text for hours, simply saying "I'm sorry Jess, I just don't know."

I later realized it was because he had to wait to hear from Scott as to what excuse he should give me. I only know what I was told, of course, but from my understanding, he was still in a relationship with Vegas girl for a couple of months after David was born. It was such an odd place to be, being a new mom again, celebrating the brand-new life we created, but doing it all on my own, even though Scott was physically there too. Eventually, I think Vegas girl broke up with him and he was forced to mope around our house. He still lived with us and still wanted me to act like a married couple, but he wouldn't give anything of himself to me or our children.

He was angry about the loss of the relationship with Vegas girl, angry that there was even less of me to give to him, and angry at the boys for taking his life as he knew it away from him. I continued to sleep downstairs in the guest bedroom next to the boys' rooms because I couldn't stand to be in the same space with him. This was definitely the lowest point in my life thus far. I had absolutely no self-worth and absolutely no one to turn to. I didn't have a single friend or family member I felt I could ask for help and I was completely alone, mostly by my own doing. I couldn't face anyone to tell them what had been happening, what I was going through; I was too embarrassed by myself for being in this position and of Scott's actions. I just went on with my day, staying clear of Scott until he left for work.

I can't explain why I was still living there, or why I hadn't sent him packing. I was so used to his behavior, yet it continued to get worse. I had allowed him to create our (my) world for so long that I wasn't capable of making things happen for myself. I hadn't told anyone of the current state of our marriage, and I didn't feel like I could ask anyone else for help. It was my inner turmoil that said, *This is your husband, no one needs to know about your drama. People will think you're weak and wonder why you put up with it for so long. What if it gets better? They'll forever hate him.*

After maternity leave was over, I went back to work for two months before it was too much work to manage Joey's school schedule with a newborn, and Scott said I should quit my job, again. We had a nanny that summer, but he was going to college in the fall, and with our previous daycare struggles, it only made sense for me to be home. This meant that I didn't have an income, causing me to rely on Scott even more. We continued to live in the same house, but only now I stayed in the guest bedroom downstairs while Scott came and went as he pleased.

Occasionally, when he needed to show someone he had a wife, we'd go out to dinner with another couple or co-workers of his and he'd ask me to put the bill on my credit card, with the assumption that he'd expense it later. We didn't share any bank accounts or credit cards, so I relied on him to pay me so that I could pay the cards we'd put money on for everything - his work dinners and events, gas for my car, groceries, etc. Each month, my credit card bills kept increasing, yet he would only give me just enough to make the minimum payments.

Checking out at the grocery store was anxiety-inducing for me. I'd reach into my purse for a credit card to pay with and would instantly start sweating. I could feel the acid filling up my stomach and my mouth would go sour. Would there be enough available credit for me to charge the groceries? Would my card get declined, forcing me to embarrassingly try another? When I asked for more money to pay off the debt, he'd tell me to just open another credit card. Scott had no qualms about spending his money on lavish things for himself but could not fathom having to spend that money on petty things like groceries for his kids.

November came, and David was about four months old when Scott met Katherine. She was a client of his, and he helped her with her mortgage when she bought her home; they'd hit it off.

Scott had left his Facebook and email accounts as "always logged in" on the home computer, and I came across it by accident when I was checking my own account. There was no way I couldn't look! I found several email and Facebook exchanges between Scott and Katherine and the stuff I would find was sickening. My stomach churned over and over, and I ran to the bathroom to expel the disgusting feeling. They thought they were in love, and it was clear by the number of times they told each other. They'd also been spending a lot of time together, going to the beach, meeting for drinks, and meeting each other's friends. So many of the messages were sent while we were together as a family, and I wondered how he could live such a separate life while in the one he was currently in. But he'd been doing it for an entire year already, so he was used to creating lies and deceit.

They knew each other for months before Katherine found out he even had a second son, and that was through a Facebook post that I tagged him in. Of course, she only knew what he told her, so I can only imagine how he spun a lie to make it ok that she didn't know about David. When people hear my story, they always ask how she could stay with him, after catching him in such a big lie, and I always say that I understand; that I have no idea why or how I stayed with him either. I didn't even blame her for staying in the relationship once she found out he was still married. I knew his manipulation and mind-bending lies all too well to know that she didn't know the truth about anything.

At the same time he was dating her, he was also doing online chats with girls that wanted help paying for breast implants, or visiting "friend-finder" websites. I could see all of this in his email account. I visited the porn sites he subscribed to and knowing his common password, I logged in to see just exactly what he was doing on there. What I found was nauseating. His obsession with women and sex was right there for me to see and my whole body became numb, tingling with shame and disgust. I felt my blood run hot throughout, and I swallowed down the vomit begging to be expelled. Not only was he expecting me to engage in constant sexting and real sex at home, but he was also paying for his fix via multiple websites, daily. Now I was faced with the information that he chose to spend his money on other women, on sex, rather than his own family.

He was obsessed with sex and needed his fix any way he could get it. Occasionally, he would come down to my bedroom and joke around, asking me what my plans for the day were like he cared. Or he'd ask for sex, coming to dry hump me from behind. I had started going to the gym nearly every day, just for something to do and because I got a couple of hours of free childcare, and by the time David was about six or seven months old, I weighed less than I had in high school, about 115 pounds on my 5'6" frame. I started losing a lot of weight from the stress of everything going on, which in turn made me more attractive to Scott. He couldn't stand that he couldn't have me, and it infuriated him. While he never physically held me down to force me to have sex with him, he mentally did. The five-ten minutes of being a complacent participant in sex were better than being called a "fucking bitch" or the unknowns of what he would do if I declined. So it continued. He continued to see Katherine and stay with her, not coming home for days, while I continued to find all the evidence and do *nothing* but endure it.

The Back Room of the Funeral

D avid was a few months old when my Papa passed away. Joey will say that it was only *his* Papa since David wasn't around long enough to know him as a grandpa. Funny how little minds work sometimes.

Dad's dad, my Papa, and I were not that close. Mom's dad had died before she was born and her stepdad died when I was very young, so Papa was the only grandpa I knew. As a little girl, my Nonnie and Papa would take my next youngest sister, Marie, and me on weekend overnights just to spend time with us. Sometimes I would go alone and sometimes I'd bring my girlfriends. Nonnie treasured having us around and loved taking care of us, and we adored her too. Papa was always there too and was certainly a kind presence, we just didn't *click* the way I did with my Nonnie.

He was an engineer and was always making lists and tinkering with building things in the garage. One of the most treasured mementos I have from Papa is a wooden crayon holder that he designed and made when I was probably in kindergarten. It's just a block of wood, with about 24 holes drilled into the top, enough for a box of crayons, in a wavy pattern so that each crayon could be seen when looking at it from any angle. He sanded it, stained it a rich cherry color, and rounded the edges of the block so that it was smooth and finished. I still have that crayon block and used it when my kids were little; I can't wait to give it to their kids someday!

When I was in college and living on my own, Papa made me a stand for my stereo that included a drawer perfectly sized and spaced for six CD cases. Since then, it has been used as a fish-tank stand for Joey's room and is now residing in a corner nook of the upstairs hallway in our new home. I love that I can say my Papa built that for me, and I can remember him fondly, sharing these stories with my kids.

Papa's funeral happened during one of the lowest points in my life. I had a new baby, a preschooler that was off the rails nearly 100% of the time, and a husband that didn't give a shit about any of us, loathing the fact that he had to spend time with us and my family at the funeral. During the service, David started fussing, so I got up to take him to the back room where I could still hear from the speakers in the ceiling. As I stood up to walk away, Scott told me I should take Joey too, because he didn't want to have to take care of him. I rolled my eyes, took Joey's hand, and ushered the three of us out of the pew and down the aisle to exit the funeral room.

Here I was, at my grandpa's funeral, experiencing it from a speaker overhead in a closed-off room with no viewing window, while my husband sat by himself with the rest of my family. I couldn't fathom why he hadn't come to take my place and let me be the one to participate, but he never came to join us. I was alone with my two boys in a giant empty room, walking around with David trying to get him to fall asleep while answering the endless questions from my four-year-old.

My resentment grew with each passing minute that Scott didn't come back to take over, or at least join me. I gave up trying to hear what was happening at the service anymore, fighting back the tears that crept in over and over. "Why isn't anyone coming to my rescue? Why am I always alone?" I screamed internally to myself, trying to still be gentle in my responses Joey.

By the time the funeral was over, it took everything I had to say my goodbyes and condolences without making a scene before ushering my little family into the car. As soon as the car doors closed, I laid into Scott with exactly how horrible I felt toward him for making me miss my own grandfather's funeral.

"How could you do that to me? How could you make me sit alone in that room by myself?"

He responded, "Who cares? You still got to listen, didn't you?" The same old response – "who cares."

I couldn't hold back my anger anymore and kept at it. "I care! I care that I had to take care of the boys all by myself and you didn't come to check on us once!"

He was enraged that I would be upset over something "so trivial" as sitting in a cavernous room all by myself with two small boys at my own grandpa's funeral. But it wasn't just that, it was the culmination of the horrible way he'd treated us over the past year, and it was finally coming out.

He kept laughing at me for being angry with him, and he was telling me I was "crazy."

"You're nuts!" he told me, "Who would get this mad over having to take their own kids out of a funeral when they're too wild to sit through it?"

We were supposed to go with my extended family to a gathering at a restaurant afterward, but we didn't go. Scott felt that I didn't deserve to go because of my "attitude." I was sobbing and full of hatred and at that moment I just wanted to get home and be away from him, so I didn't fight him.

I didn't tell anyone what happened that day. I might have, later, but at the time, these were things that I knew weren't right and knew shouldn't be ok, but didn't want people judging my relationship. I know it's wrong, I don't need you to tell me it's wrong and then expect me to do something about it. What *could* I do?

Standing up for myself only led to fights and he'd spin it so that I was the bad person instead, every single time. I stopped even trying, just let it go, disappointment after disappointment.

By my grandpa's funeral, he had been having affair after affair, and we hadn't even figured out how we would be moving forward with our relationship. We were mostly just living together and tolerating each other, so why did he feel like he even belonged amongst my family? Why did he *want* to sit and mourn with the others when he was one foot out the door anyway? Because none of them knew what was happening with us. Because he lived his life as though it were two separate worlds – the one with us and the one with *her*; *the* collective "her" for which he was trying to find happiness outside of himself. He wanted to have his cake and eat it too, and I was a complicit accomplice allowing the madness to continue.

Vodka and Cigarettes

I don't remember much of David's first year. Joey was in special education preschool every day and was a handful to manage at home. I had a brand-new baby and a really angry and absent husband. I just remember feeling like I was waiting for him to decide to leave, to move in with his girlfriend. I didn't have the ability to ask him to leave, mentally or physically. He held all the power in our relationship; even if I had asked him to leave, I didn't know the reaction I would have faced. Even though he never hit me, I feared him; I feared what he would do to me or our boys.

It was always in subtle ways that should have been obvious and deserved more attention but were easy to brush off as "caught up in the moment" *things*. One Christmas, when Joey was small, he had been wandering around jabbering non-stop as usual, when Scott got irritated and pushed him out of the way. Joey fell and started crying, and Scott started yelling at me.

I rushed over to Joey, overcome with emotion myself at seeing this situation play out, scooped him up, and headed to the garage to get us out of there. I didn't even stop to put on shoes, and the garage was heated so the car would be warm enough to not need coats. It was early evening and near Joey's bedtime, so I drove us around to look at Christmas lights in any neighborhood I could find, not going back home for nearly two hours.

I would be so angry one minute, wondering how Scott could behave that way, to do that to Joey and yell at me for his own behavior. And then my eyes would fill with tears, my throat choking up wondering why the hell I was in a position to need to get my son out of the house and away from his father. The Christmas lights were only a reminder of the special season we were in, full of family and happiness.

When I think of domestic abuse, I think of the physical acts, the visible things, and the things you cannot hide. I cannot even fathom being subject to this kind of abuse, having to endure beatings and black eyes, or being threatened with objects. However, there are other forms of abuse that are equally as damaging and painful in unique ways. While I never suffered a noticeable mark, I was subject to physical abuse by having objects thrown at my head, just close enough to not actually hit me. Scott would destroy my property just because he was upset, and I "deserved" it. I was forced to engage in sex with him because it was my "wifely duty" and the only way he knew how to show me his love. My children were pushed and pulled with more force than necessary for the given situation, if it even called for any physical movement at all.

Emotional abuse and manipulation can be hard to recognize and are often brushed off as just a personality trait. Even now, I find myself questioning, "Was it really that bad? What about all of those women that are actually, *physically* abused? They're the ones needing to be saved, to be taken care of and removed from awful situations!"

While this is true, and the weight of sadness I feel for all of those women, and men, and *children* that are violently abused at home crushes me, abuse doesn't have to be violent to be happening. People can go on masquerading as if they live a perfect life, "fortunate even," but who did they step on to get there?

One morning, while feeding the boys breakfast, I suddenly heard a loud crashing sound coming from the stairs down the hall. I stared at the kids, wondering what had just happened when I heard it again. I picked David up and walked over to the stairs to find Scott standing at the top holding a box of my mom's china we had been storing for her. I looked down the stairs to find the other box already at the bottom, smashed. I looked back at Scott in shock, to see him lifting the box in the air and throwing it down the stairs to meet the other.

"What are you doing?" I screamed at him, trying to rush to stop him, unsuccessfully as I was still holding David.

"Don't you dare touch me while holding our son." he sneered back.

I was in panic mode, not understanding what was happening. Why was he throwing my mom's china down the stairs, over and over? Why was he so upset? I didn't know how to make it stop, and thankfully, Scott walked right past me and left for work. Again, I was left crying to pick up the mess he'd created.

It turns out, I had woken Scott up in the middle of the night because I was talking in my sleep. He woke up to find me sitting up in bed, talking nonsense to the ceiling fan, and it freaked him out. He said that he slapped my face to get me to wake up and told me to go back to sleep, which apparently worked, but he had then been too scared to fall back asleep. The family legend about Mom's china was that it was bought at an auction from a haunted house. Scott thought that my random sleep talking episode was surely a product of ghostly spirits brought to our house from china, and therefore it must be destroyed.

I have never told this story to my family, and nearly ten years later, I will need to since I've written it here. I was horrified and too ashamed to tell Mom what had happened; that because of me, her china had been ruined. I also couldn't face the wrath of Scott if I had told her, which would cause my family to be upset with him. I knew he'd blame me, "You're the one who was possessed!"

136

After the incident, I sifted through the boxes to see what could be salvaged. For those that couldn't be, I did my best to find replacement pieces online, but it got to be too time-consuming and expensive that I eventually gave up. Every time I went to open those boxes, I was again faced with the realization that horrible things were being done to me, but I couldn't tell anyone about it. I would rather spend hours and hours looking for replacement pieces than tell anyone what had happened to avoid others' suffering.

Scott finally moved out of our home and in with Katherine in June, a month before David's first birthday. There was no discussion about it, no official "I'm moving out," he was just no longer popping in and out of our house anymore. I felt free, no longer burdened by his sometimes there, mostly not, attitude. I no longer had to be surprised by hearing the garage door open, running into my room to pretend to be asleep, just so that I didn't have to interact with him.

I was relieved but also tormented. As he was leaving one day I said, "I can't wait for the day that you get bored with her and move onto the next!"

It was a way to say, "good riddance" and that I knew he thought he was leaving to greener grass, but that it wouldn't last.

He responded, simply, "I would never cheat on her; she's perfect."

He said it without saying it, "You are not worth it and it's your fault I'm leaving for someone better."

Spoiler alert! He did cheat on her, and they got divorced after only having been married about two years. He was engaged to a new mistress not even a year later. Third time's a charm? Doubt it.

Scott insisted I call her Katherine, even though everyone she knew called her Kat. Her name on social media was Kat, and that was clearly her preferred name; until she met Scott, of course. Shortly after they moved in together officially, she quit her important day job to work with Scott. The pattern of his coercive control was obvious to me from the start, even if it went unnoticed by most. She's like me, except she's not. She was me when I was young, before kids, able to devote her entire self to him. She was independently successful when she met him, caring, trusting, and beautiful. Kat was exactly the perfect victim once he had discarded me.

After the boys were in bed for the night, I'd pour myself a shot or two of vodka to try to numb the hurt. Every night I stood in front of the open door to the patio while smoking a single cigarette. I couldn't believe this was my life. I didn't even smoke, and I only drank during social occasions, but there I was, sitting in the kitchen alone, sobbing with no one to talk to; no one to tell me it would be ok or what I should do now.

Once the vodka kicked in to relax my overly stressed nerves and I was exhausted from crying, I would fall asleep and wake up bright and early to do it all over again. I wasn't new to being the sole provider for the boys and the household duties, and it was a relief to not have him coming around anymore.

In July, Scott's parents hosted a poolside first birthday party for David at their house, and it was the first time Scott and I had to interact since he had moved out. Both of our immediate families were there, including the boys' godparents. We hadn't yet told anyone about what was going on, not that he had moved out of our house and into his girlfriend's, and not that he had been having affairs for the last two years (at least). They had no idea that we were no longer speaking. We tried to act civilly toward each other, but he was horrible to me without anyone else noticing, and I avoided being in his space the entire day.

Scott was in the pool with Joey while I was on the edge with David, and he'd swim near me just to say, "You're such a bitch," while smiling and laughing like we were sharing a joke. I got up and walked away, refusing to take his bait.

After the party, I took the boys back home and that was about the last time he showed interest in the boys for months, outside of a few brief visits at our house. He called it "babysitting" and he'd offer to come over and babysit so I could go out on dates. He took a fascination in getting me to date other men; he wanted to hear the stories and what sexual activities we'd partake in. It was disgusting. I wasn't even dating! How could I possibly find the mental capacity to give any part of me to another individual. I took his babysitting time to just drive, go to Target, or run errands.

I always knew when Kat wasn't home when the boys were with Scott. He would incessantly text me, about the boys or about what I was doing with my alone time. He couldn't bear to be alone. One Saturday night he started texting me about David being sick and he didn't know what to do. He kept texting over and over and I was getting worried. I texted Kat, asking if she was home, and she responded that she wasn't, but would be soon. I was relieved, knowing that help was on the way. She didn't have kids of her own, but she was the one to do most of the parenting between the two of them. Scott had told me at the beginning of their relationship that she had said, "I hope I meet your kids and they make me not want to have kids." I thought it was such an odd thing to say, if she even said it at all, and even weirder for him to tell me.

A few days after David's birthday party, I went over to Mom's house to finally tell her what was going on with me and Scott. He had officially moved out and there was no denying we needed to get a divorce. The boys played in the other room while she and I sat on opposite couches in her living room. It was the middle of the day and she offered me a glass of wine, but I declined.

"I have to tell you what's been going on with me and Scott." I started.

"Alright," she said, "Is everything ok?"

"Well, no, not really at all. He moved out about six weeks ago and has been living with his girlfriend." I calmly explained what had been happening over the past couple of years and where we were currently at in our relationship. I didn't show much emotion at all, and I found I didn't have much either. I stated the facts as they had happened, and that I was now on my own. I didn't have a plan for what was going to happen, other than I assumed we'd be moving out of our house.

"I have to ask you a question," she said calmly.

"Ok," I responded.

"Are you taking drugs?" I couldn't help but laugh, but she was stone-faced serious.

She continued, "Seriously, Jess, are you on drugs?"

I couldn't believe she was asking me this! I had no idea where she was coming from with this question, and I was offended that she asked. I responded, defensively, "No, I'm not on drugs! What do you mean and why are you asking me that?"

Her voice calm yet confused, she asked, "How on earth are you coping with all of this?"

I relaxed when I realized that she was complimenting me, rather than accusing me. I didn't ask, but I'm (almost) certain that she meant antidepressants rather than cocaine or something. I think she would have understood if I had, in either scenario. I was not taking medication of any kind, and I think I was so used to functioning while numb that it became my normal state.

Now that it was out in the open, I needed to *do* something about it. I couldn't just go on waiting for whatever it was to be done to me, to my life. I had recently begun trying to connect with one of my girlfriends from college; she was a bridesmaid in our wedding, and she knew the history of my relationship with Scott. Her mom was a local law librarian and recommended an attorney, which was something I had no idea how to go about finding. Mom came with me to the initial consultation, as she had gone through her own divorce from my dad years before so she was somewhat familiar with the process and what would need to be done. She was in full mama-bear mode and wanted to fight for me, except I wouldn't let her. She didn't know Scott like I did, and I wanted as little conflict as possible. I just wanted to be done with him and move on.

I told the attorney, Julie, the details of the current state of Scott and my relationship, including our financial situation. To me, the information I was providing seemed factual and just my life, but at one point I noticed Julie and my mom glance at each other with a look that suggested horror/sadness/helplessness. They seemed to not know how to process the details they'd been given, therefore taking my direction of just getting "it" done, whatever that would be.

To come up with the value of my personal belongings, Mom took me to a pawn shop to get a low-ball value of my engagement ring, which turned out to be unnecessary anyway. A few mornings later I noticed that my ring was no longer where I'd kept it. When I asked Scott about it, he told me he sold it; just like that.

"Why should *you* get it," he asked me, "I'm the one that bought it! It's mine."

Not long after the ring went missing, he texted me to let me know that a tow truck would be coming to pick up my SUV because he had sold that too, which would leave me without a vehicle.

"You can't just take away my mode of transportation!" I replied, continuing, "How are the boys and I supposed to go anywhere?"

His response was, "You should have thought of that when filing for divorce. You can't afford the BMW anyway, why would you want it?"

I immediately called my attorney for advice. She told me to take the vehicle and hide out at a friend's house for a few days while we figured out what to do. So, I did; I took the boys and the

SUV to an old friend's house to have a slumber party with her and her two young girls. We camped out and made the best of the crazy situation we were in.

Scott was pissed because he missed the opportunity with the buyer and would "just have to try again." He had gotten his own lawyer by then and was informed that he wouldn't be able to take the vehicle away from me and our kids, so I was able to keep it for a couple more months until I found something for myself.

Scott's uncle, Mike, had been our financial planner for a while until Scott burned too many business bridges with him and was fired as a client. Mike had agreed to keep me on as a client and when another client's spouse passed away, leaving a very well cared for used vehicle that was in my budget, Mike set up the sale. Things were looking up!

Now that I wasn't getting consistent support from him and didn't know what my future held, I had to get a job. I met a friend, Harper, for a sushi lunch with David while Joey was at preschool. Harper and I were sitting in a booth across from each other with David in his highchair next to us. She was a work friend from my previous job, and we'd become close through her training me. I had taken over her role at the company I worked for after things got difficult at home with Joey, and she wanted to tell me about a position that opened up where she currently worked.

"It's a pretty cushy position," Harper said, "and you'll be doing a lot of the same work you did at your last job. I think this would be a great fit for you, and I love the company; they treat us well."

I'm sold! I knew I wasn't in a position to be picky about a job, and this sounded like a great opportunity just falling into my lap.

We spent the rest of our lunch chatting about life, my boys, and how I'm handling things with Scott. When the bill came, I reached in my purse for my credit card and saw I had several messages on my cell. There were missed calls from daycare, a few from Scott, and a bunch of texts from him as well.

He was frantic about something, texting, "What is wrong with you? Where the hell are you? Our son is at daycare and you don't monitor your phone? You need to call me now!"

Except, I didn't call him right away; I first called daycare to see what had happened, panicked that there might have been some accident.

"Oh, hi, thanks for calling me back," the daycare mom said, in a much calmer tone than expected. "Joey stuck some peas up his nose at lunch. I think I got them all out, but I don't know how many he put up there, so I would feel better if you took him in to the pediatrician to have him checked out."

I was annoyed. I was annoyed that I couldn't even enjoy one leisurely lunch with a girlfriend, a child in tow, without an incident. An incident that should have been a simple relay of information – peas up the nose, probably should get it checked out, just in case – yet I was berated for having been so *careless* as to not check my phone for what amounted to about thirty minutes.

The daycare mom had called Scott after she couldn't reach me and given that he had no idea how kids behave, or what to do if anything should happen, he was upset with me that he had to even deal with it at all. And what he had to deal with, was to answer a phone call from daycare and receive information about his child being a child.

After it was settled that I needed to go pick Joey up and take him in to get checked out, Harper and I said our goodbyes, and I assured her that I wanted to apply for the position. I knew the job required some travel to the San Francisco headquarters, which I truly didn't know how I would make work but knew that this was an opportunity I couldn't pass up; a job with great pay and great hours for my new role as a single mom to two young kiddos.

I guess I really shouldn't say new role since I had been a single parent all along, but I was so grateful to the universe that this job fell into my lap. I was finally on my own, in my own space with the right to make my own decisions. I felt the greatest sense of relief and finally had room to breathe. Instead of feeling despair for all the things that were lost, I felt hopeful that I could finally start living *my* life.

It was this job that would allow me to pay off the twenty-grand in credit card debt that Scott left me with, most of it from fancy work dinners out, groceries, utilities, and basic necessities. Since the cards were in my name only, and he convinced me that this "minimal" amount of debt was surely better than splitting the debt he carried, I agreed to take it in our divorce.

On top of a fantastic job opportunity, I found a townhouse to rent about five miles away from where the boys were born, in the same school district they would have gone to if we had stayed. It was freshly remodeled, and we were the first renters for the new owners. There were three bedrooms, three bathrooms, and enough room for us to start to heal as a little family of three. Except I wasn't free of the weight of his hold just yet. I still didn't have a support network and people I could ask for help, and I still needed his opinion and approval for where we would live. I mean, I *didn't* need it, but my manipulated mind relied so much on him telling me what to do, that I still needed him to tell me it was ok, to approve of my choice.

I asked Scott to tour the house with me, which he did willingly; he enjoyed that I still depended on him. As we were walking through the bedrooms upstairs he said, mocking me, in the way he did with everyone when he wanted you to know that he was better than you, "Well, isn't this a nice big place for just the three of you!" As in, "I think this is too nice and I wanted you to suffer a little more than this." But he didn't have much of a choice, he had validated for me that this was a nice place, and we would do well here.

Scott helped me find some movers off of Craigslist and helped monitor them back and forth from the old house to the new. He took pride in being the one that could set all of this up for poor, little old me. I suppose you could look at this gesture as kindness, that he wanted to take care of us, and maybe part of him did. It's these moments that made me question the bad stuff – "He *is* a nice guy though! He didn't have to help us move..."

And then I'm left responding with niceness too, thinking "Here's the guy I know! We're friends, not enemies." It's these moments, which were seemingly far more frequent than the bad ones, that pulled me in only to have me become a victim again to the mental and emotional abuse.

I took all the furniture from our old house that would fit into the new one and tried to make it our new home. He didn't want anything but the master bedroom set, which I wasn't going to put up a fight over. David was only a toddler and still in his crib with the changing table/dresser combo, and Joey had his bunk bed. I took the bed frame and mattress from our spare room at the old house, which was Scott's from high school and certainly in need of tossing, but it's all we had available. I took two couches for my two living rooms and then the kitchen table set. My landlord helped me hang the TVs, to ensure I didn't ruin the walls by doing it myself.

There was a little loft upstairs between the three bedrooms, and I put a TV there with a couch and a reading nook for the boys. It was a cozy place to sit and cuddle while watching a movie or reading a book before bed. We also had a living room off the kitchen on the main level, with a gas fireplace for our stockings at Christmas. It was there that we'd often turn music on the TV and have dance parties or watch cartoons in the morning. It was also there that I'd spend nearly an entire day during the occasional day or two when Scott would take them, endlessly watching TV or movie marathons, needing that time to rest my mind and body.

Behind the living room, next to the kitchen, there was a storage area under the stairs that I made into the boys' toy storage/playroom. They had all of their stuffed animals, toys, cars, and games stashed away in there, and it was the perfect size for them to run in and out of. Occasionally, nearly the entire inventory of toys and playthings would end up strewn about the main floor and I wouldn't have the energy to have them clean it up, but it worked for us, and we were happy, free.

I finally didn't have to worry about Scott coming home to see a mess, and sometimes I left dishes in the sink until the next day just because I could. Nothing was expected of me, and every choice I made was mine to make. It was certainly overwhelming at times, knowing that I was responsible for all of the bills and household decisions, but it mostly felt freaking fantastic.

Breaking Up is Hard to Do

How can you possibly find happiness alone when the only happiness you've known was with someone that made you miserable? I didn't really know I was miserable; I mean, I guess at some level I did, but getting divorced isn't something you're supposed to do after you make vows with someone. And it's especially not something you do when you have children together, or at least that's how society made me feel.

Although we had only been married for six years by the time he moved out, we'd been a couple for thirteen. I grew up with him. I'd spent my entire early adulthood with him and most of what I learned about being in a relationship was through him. It's really easy to look from the outside in and see signs, or question things that seem odd; but when you're in it, it's easy to have blinders on and make excuses, both to yourself and others.

I can't remember much of the good stuff, the things that kept me wanting to be with him; there's been too much bad in between. But there must have been, there had to have been good. We were friends, lovers, but we were not in love and I know that now. Sometimes I look back and think that he showed me how to be an adult; he replaced my parents as soon as I moved out for college. He taught me how to drive a stick shift, how to host a party, and how to want more out of life.

People will ask me why I stayed with him, and why others didn't show me the light. I stayed with him because he was my best friend, because we had a lot of fun together and because I didn't know any better. He was fun and boisterous and funny, and people seemed to enjoy being around him. Except, I know now that they didn't. I have had numerous friends and family members tell me how much they disliked him then, and still to this day. I've had people reach out to me for an honest opinion of his character. They know something seems off, he's boastful and careless, but they also see his success. "I've heard this, could it be true?" This has come in the form of protection, protecting others they know from getting into potentially bad situations with him. I spoke honestly, but carefully, it's not my place. I don't know who he is today, only what I've experienced in my own way.

Others didn't say anything because most people don't want to meddle in other people's relationships. Or they thought they'd said their peace, but it fell on the deaf ears of a girl that thought she was in love. Also, they didn't even know there was anything wrong because I was too embarrassed to share the details. The embarrassment represented shame, and I didn't want to be shamed for falling in love with him. I've since learned that I had no idea what it meant to be loved.

I didn't tell people about our problems; I knew that the things he was doing were wrong, but I felt like I had to protect him, as my husband. I felt embarrassed and ashamed, but I didn't feel like there was anything anyone could do, and that sharing the things that were happening would only have people get upset with him which would make my life miserable. What I understand now is that even if I did everything right and he was happy, he wasn't genuinely happy because he can never have enough. I wasn't doing myself any favors by hiding the truth.

The thing was, I didn't see divorce as an option myself. That's part of the reason I stayed, because they say marriage is tough and everyone goes through hard times. I thought that was the case for us, that these were just the hard times and that once the kids were older, we'd find our groove again. That someday we would be happy again; or at least that I would be. I have always been thankful that he made the choice for us to get divorced. Even though I was the one to file the divorce papers, he had already been living with his girlfriend and I figured there was no going back.

After he moved out, I didn't want to stay in the house, nor could I afford to. He didn't want to move back into our family home because he knew what the neighbors thought of him and he didn't want to deal with that. He couldn't sell it because it was so far under water financially and he certainly couldn't let it go into foreclosure as that would cause him to lose his business license, and therefore his livelihood. So, he had no other choice but to rent it out.

I gave him that house in the divorce because there was so much negative equity and I wanted nothing to do with it. He got us into that whole mess, and he could be left to deal with the aftermath. He needed the big, expensive house we couldn't afford, and he was unfaithful in all aspects of our marriage, it was the least I could do for him.

As part of our divorce decree, I needed to sign a quit claim deed to remove myself from the title. I signed the paperwork and gave it to Scott to file. He didn't get around to filing it for a year or so, and eventually asked me to sign another copy. He gave me the address of where I was to go to sign the new paperwork, and as I was walking into the building he called me to give me better directions to the office.

"Remember the girl that gave us the clap? Erika? Well, she's the one that'll have the document for you to sign." He laughed about it like it was the funniest thing he'd heard that day.

I was mortified. I started to sweat and could feel the blood leave my face. *I've never had the clap. What is he talking about?* And then I remembered; around the same time as the "drug friend" situation years ago, he had told me a story about a friend of his that snuck antibiotics into his girlfriend's food when he found out he had gotten an STD. It had been a joke, a story that he had heard, and he said, "Isn't that crazy? Can you even imagine?" I can't imagine, no, and I can't believe this story was his own, ours, all along. He had gotten an STD and rather than tell me about it, he got treatment for it, secretly treating me as well.

I debated turning around, saying "Screw you, figure out how to do this on your own," but I didn't. Why not? Why did I continuously just do whatever he asked of me? I paced back and forth in the lobby by the elevators, finally taking them to the fourth floor as directed. Again, once I got off the elevators I paced, so angry and embarrassed. Does she know who I am? Does she remember this situation? Of course, she wouldn't; she wouldn't have known he had a girlfriend at the time, nor that I was his now ex-wife! But I didn't think logically at that moment - I was far too embarrassed and upset.

I decided I wanted to get out of there as fast as I could, so I opened the door to their office and let them know I was there to sign the paperwork. I have no idea if the woman helping me was Erika, I just know I signed as fast as I could, nearly running the rest of the way to my car where I sat, once again crying over my own stupidity.

Even though he left us for Katherine, it took about two years for Scott to stop asking for pictures of my boobs or asking for details of my intimate relationships as tools for his sexual fantasies. I never obliged, but that didn't stop him from asking. At least once a week I'd get texts from him practically begging me to "help him out," which meant he wanted sexual favors. After I was moved out and on my own, I was still pulled into his madness. Six months after he moved in with Kat, the following text exchange took place:

12/20 at 4:17 pm: *Can you just tell me how much bigger it is?*

He thought I was dating and wanted to know how big the guy's penis was. Not only was he curious about this fact, but he also wanted me to talk about it with him! He *wanted* me to tell him that I was out banging some guy with a huge dick as some way to get back at him.

12/20 at 4:23 pm: *Just be nice and text. If you text for 10 mins, I will meet up and help you with bills. This is fair.*

I had previously told him that I didn't have money to pay for daycare or groceries and that all of my credit cards were maxed out because he had stopped supporting us. But for him to support his (still) wife and kids I had to "satisfy" him. I knew enough that he would not live up to his end of the bargain so I would not give in to his requests.

My response at 4:27 pm was *"No. I'm sorry."*

This is fair. That is how it was, he dictated to me what was fair, told me how I should feel about things. Over time I became numb to my own feelings. I complied without question because I had lost my sense of self in the manipulation.

He spent the next two hours texting me and again for hours the next morning.

12/21 at 12:02 pm: *I want to leave you alone, but you have to tell me something. It makes it worse when you don't answer. Can you give me 5 mins please and I won't text you again today?*

What I have learned since is to not respond at all. As with everything with him, give him an inch and he'll take a mile, so I went silent. Every text came through as if he hadn't yet sent one, just reiterating that he wanted me to sext with him. What I know now is that he could not stand that he didn't have control over me anymore and that I wasn't his. He would look for a connection in any way he could, and for him, sex was love. He had often told me that, that to feel close to me or to "love" me, he needed to have sex with me. Unfortunately, I learned too late that love and intimacy do not develop, nor are they maintained, simply from a sexual connection.

As he was my first love, that's what he taught me about how a relationship should work. The demise of our marriage was because he is incapable of love, of finding joy and happiness in life's special moments. He sees people for what they can do for him, and when they can't fill his needs, they're worthless to him. His children turned *his* wife into a mother and someone he now had to share, and our children were obstacles to his joy and happiness.

Gold Digger

"Mama, why did Dad throw our bags into the street?" Joey's little voice asked.

I tried to sound cheerful, replying, "I'm not sure buddy! But that's ok, I'll get them as soon as I finish buckling you guys in."

Scott and I had been divorced for a year, but the abuse hadn't let up. He no longer had me to control, fueling his anger and resentment toward me.

For the first time in many years, I went on a girlfriend's weekend away with some friends from work. It was the middle of January, the air cold and snowy, the perfect weather to be cozied up in a cabin with girlfriends, drinking coffee until it was time for wine. But Sunday morning came quickly, and we were on the road by noon, planning to be home for the scheduled 4 pm kid exchange with Scott.

I had informed Scott well in advance that we would be an hour later than originally discussed, as we had run into some traffic and delays from the snow, but he insisted on showing up at the meeting place at the original time. He waited, with the boys in the car, for an hour until I got there, incessantly texting me, asking when I'd be there, even though I'd already told him – 5 o'clock.

As soon as I pulled my car in front of his to park, he got out, grabbed their bags, and threw them as far into the street as he could manage, leaving them there for me to pick up from the damp pavement. It was dark by then, the winter skies hazy in the streetlights. He wouldn't speak to me or even acknowledge that I was there, other than to show me he was upset through silent treatment and hostility towards our children that I'd left in his care longer than he preferred. He got the boys out of their car seats and set them on the snowbank of the curb, getting back into his car as fast as he could. I rushed over to grab the boys, getting them safely into my car while he sped off, narrowly missing their bags lying on the road.

When I first met with Julie, my divorce attorney, she asked me what I thought the biggest point of contention would be for us in the divorce. I said, "Without a doubt, it will be the finances. Money is everything to him."

She was surprised considering that during a divorce, most people have the hardest time agreeing to the custody arrangement. I laughed at that thought and told her that there would be no argument to me having the boys full-time. He never fought me for more parenting time, other than wanting to see them less than every other weekend. I pushed an every-other-weekend parenting schedule so that the boys could still have some sort of relationship with their father. I was not going to let him just walk away from the children *we* brought into this world.

"You don't get to just wash your hands of all of us," I told him. He wanted nothing to do with any of us.

Fathers not taking care of their kids after a divorce or separation seems to be the "norm." We seem to collectively be ok with that being the expected outcome and that children are "a woman's responsibility," especially when the parents are no longer together. But why? Today's generation of parents is co-parenting happily, more than any generation before. Dads are not only expected, but are absolutely willing, to contribute to caring for and raising their children. So why is it just accepted that after a divorce it becomes the mother's job to care for the children and the dad's job to pay child support?

For a year and a half, I had to beg and plead for Scott to show an interest in the boys. I couldn't believe the man I had been with for years, the man I married and had children with, was completely okay with just walking away from it all.

After frequent visit reschedules, and last-minute "I can't pick them up tomorrow," notices, I sent him the following in an email:

"I think you're mean and spiteful and I'm sick of offering and begging you to spend time with our boys. If you want to see them or talk to them, you can set up a regular schedule and make it a fair routine for all of us. I'm not going to let you randomly reach out only when it's convenient for you. When you want to schedule a routine for FaceTime calls and spend time with them, let me know. Until then, I'll plan to have them 100% of the time so there aren't any letdowns."

He responded:

"Like I said before if you want 100% custody. Take them. Do not ask me for $.01. I have to have a schedule with you to FaceTime my boys? That's sick and weird." (I laugh that he took the time to make it an actual penny, rather than just say "one cent" or "a penny")

In our case, not only does he <u>not</u> want to financially support our children, but he also doesn't want time with them. He saw them at the bare minimum level to not have to pay any more in child support. This minimum amount is ten percent of the time, which amounts to thirty-six overnights a year. I am thankful that he doesn't see them more, because I can't imagine seeing them less than I do. And I'm grateful that his influence on them is minimized to every-other-weekend visits. I've heard horror stories of narcissistic parents demanding more parenting time with their kids just to avoid paying for them and then having family members or hired nannies care for them instead. All too often, the non-narcissistic parent is accused of anything and everything just to be made to look "crazy" to the courts, losing custody altogether. I have always considered myself fortunate that Scott hasn't been *that* horrible. My bad was bad, but it could've been much worse.

One year, three weeks before the end of the year, Scott hit the sixteen percent mark, or fifty-eight overnights, well above the minimum in his eyes. He sent me a text that he "had done his fair share in this relationship."

He called me a gold-digger and said that since I wanted "top dollar" for child support (which was several hundred dollars less a month than what the state recommended) he only had to see them the minimum amount of time and would not be seeing them for the rest of the year. This was the text he sent me,

"I think you forget how amazing you have it compared to other situations. With the child support that you have chosen - the decree states that I need to see the children 865 hours a year, or 72 hours a month, at a minimum. In May, I was with the boys 132 hours *(which is only 5 out of 31 days…)*. That does NOT include FaceTime. So, for you to say that I don't see my boys enough - is not a fair statement."*

Child support is determined by the state, using detailed calculations of income, parenting time, children's expenses, healthcare, daycare, etc. There is no breakdown of hours within our decree and parenting time is only calculated based on overnights. I never knew Scott as a details guy, so it was always interesting when he'd try to throw random facts at me. I knew the details of our decree and I gave up trying to explain them to him.

An email from him after submitting a medical bill for Joey's broken arm –

"That sucks. That's why you are paid $XXX a week, 52 weeks a year. If you can't afford this, please ask your friend to pay for the bill because it was her responsibility."

My friend and coworker had stayed with the boys while I was on a work trip because Scott did not want to watch them. Joey decided it would be fun to build a tower of blocks and stand on it, however, he fell off and broke his arm. My friend had to take him to the emergency room, comforting him while he had x-rays and got a cast on his arm. She took care of him while I was gone, and his father wanted no part of it. He thought I was traveling to see a boyfriend and wanted to punish me by having me find someone else to stay with the boys. Even with a broken arm involved, I was still more comfortable with my friend watching the boys than their father.

Scott believed he was superior. He felt he deserved unquestioning compliance. He was unable and unwilling to recognize the needs and feelings of others. He was able to manipulate a conversation to make himself appear like he was doing me a favor when in reality he just felt inadequate or without control. In the following email to me, he is agreeing that I have the boys a lot of the time, but he's doing far more than "every other ex-husband" by being current on his child support, which was only the case because the county had caught up with him and his paychecks were being garnished for the support. In this email, he also suggests that once he gets his business up and running, his girl-friend will be able to become a stay-at-home "mother" to our children. Lastly, he sees the divorce decree as a court order for when he *needs* to see his children, rather than a tool to make sure he *can* see them.

"I am not asking to be friends. Just a normal parenting relation-ship... if I ask for a favor, you help out and vice versa. I know you think that you are the only one raising the boys. Physically, yes.... you have the boys a lot. But you have to be a little understanding that I am helping out greatly financially. You have been paid every penny promised to you. That is a very far stretch from every other ex-husband.

Once my business gets up and running again, Katherine will be quit-ting her job to stay home, and we'll be able to take the boys more often.

Also, remember, this is what I tried to talk to you about over a year ago... when I asked you 'do you really know what being a single mother is like?'... this is the life you wanted. You wanted a life away from me and you got it.

157

Aside from seeing the boys on Wednesday nights, I see them as much as the decree states I should see them. Even the perfect father in a divorce would only see the kids 3 hours extra per week. So given the circumstances, I think that I am being a great father."

Even after being divorced for five years, I'll still receive texts from him telling me how I live such a "rough life" as a "divorced mother" when he realized he would have the boys one extra night that month. That's how he makes fun of a situation – "oh, you have it so rough!" He was mad at me because he had to have the boys one extra night in a month, which meant I would have an extra night "off."

I responded simply "313-52"; I have them three hundred and thirteen nights a year to his fifty-two. These texts just come out of nowhere for me... I mean, why is he so hell-bent on trying to make me feel guilty about an extra night away? What does calling me a "divorced mother" prove? He's a divorced father, but apparently not seeing his kids 313 nights a year doesn't affect him in the least.

The first Christmas after being separated, he had the boys overnight, yet he continued to text me. His texts to me were not about the kids, or of any sign of remorse or lost love, but rather continued requests for details of how I'd be spending the holidays with the guy he thought I was dating. He was obsessed with details and even though I never gave them to him, he'd come up with scenarios on his own and then get upset with me when I wouldn't confirm nor deny those details.

12/25: *You have the night off and I hope you take advantage. What do you have planned?*

My response: *It's really nice to just be alone and relax.*

12/25: *Why lie? So weird.*

My response: *I'm not going out. I have no plans. I don't have any friends that go out. I have 2 young kids almost full-time. I like to relax and sleep when they're gone.*

12/25: *You would get so much more from me with the truth. I am in love with Katherine and wouldn't change it for the world. I can't even imagine going through a divorce, living on your own with 2 kids, starting a new job, and going through the holidays alone.*

It's amazing how we both went through this divorce together, have two kids together, and have to split holidays with our children, yet he just can't imagine it. He does not have empathy or the ability to see something from another perspective. He has always blamed me for his affairs and our divorce and that somehow, I asked for all of this. So, my punishment is to have to do it all alone.

The toughest thing through all of the lies and deceit was his inability to own the responsibility, to admit the infractions, and apologize for the pain he'd caused. He wouldn't give me the satisfaction of validating what he'd done to me and our family. Every action and every lie he told was because of something I didn't do for him because I didn't love him enough. That's what he told me over and over.

It has been five years and I now understand that I was abused, mentally and emotionally abused, for years. I had no idea the extent of it all. Thankfully, I found support groups through social media where I could read other people's stories and know that I was not alone. Reading through their stories, so raw and real, gave me a connection that helped validate and give a name to what I was going through. Slowly, the fog began to lift, and I could understand why he behaved the way he did and still does.

Now I am armed with tools like gray rocking and the ability to not engage in his madness. With the Gray Rock Method, the intent is to be so boring and monotonous in your contact with the other person that they lose interest in engaging with you altogether. No matter how infuriating he was or how upset he'd make me with his hateful and hurtful texts, I learned to limit my interactions to only what was necessary for our boys. Those conversations would look something like this:

Me, on a Thursday before one of his weekends with the boys: *"David came down with a cold and has a little cough and runny nose."*

His response: *"Ok, thanks."*

Five minutes later he said, *"Maybe you should look into getting your carpets cleaned so he doesn't get sick."*

No response from me.

Another five minutes, *"Why are they always sick? Maybe you should find a new daycare."*

Still no response from me.

"Seriously, don't you think it's weird that one of them is always sick?"

Finally, he gave up; I wasn't taking the bait and he's not getting anything from me, so he just stopped. If I were to engage and try to explain or defend myself, he would keep going, digging deeper, and in the end, he would win; I'd be a sobbing mess, doubting myself as the sole caregiver of my children.

I lived in a newly remodeled townhome with brand new carpet and flooring, why would my carpet need to be cleaned? Yet, his incessant jabs got to me. I had David allergy tested to see if there was, in fact, something wrong with him. But he was just a toddler in daycare full time who caught a few colds each winter.

"Maybe you should find a new daycare…" As with everything, the sole responsibility for the boys' well-being was mine. I *loved* our daycare provider. She was simply amazing and made me feel ok with leaving my boys in her care while I worked.

The days (and oftentimes nights) were incredibly long. Waking early to get the boys ready for daycare was sometimes the hardest part of the day - getting everyone dressed, fed, lunches made and packed with two young boys running about the house doing the exact opposite of what you've asked them to do. I think every working parent that does daycare drop-offs knows the drive to work after dropping them at daycare is about the most peaceful and serene part of the day. Seriously! It's silent, outside of the ringing in your ears from the previous hour (or two) of incessant child chatter and squeals and demands to "get your *shoes* on." On more than one occasion I got all the way to work without realizing I never turned the radio on. Blissful silence.

But there were also brilliantly bright moments in between the chaos. One morning, I came downstairs after getting myself ready to find the youngest in the highchair with the biggest bowl of Kix cereal on his tray. The bowl was filled to the brim with milk and the little golden balls of cornmeal goodness and in his hand was an oversized spoon with a ginormous grin on his sweet little face. His brother had gotten him up into his chair, fastened him in, and served him breakfast. It. Was. Adorable.

These were the moments that made the never-ending days tolerable, and I continued to look for them. Even with these adorable moments, the days became countdowns to when they'd go to dad's again and I'd finally get a break. A Monday after a weekend with my boys became only four more days until I could lie on the couch and think of nothing else but the movie marathon I would watch for the weekend and rest.

I Can't Take Care of You, Too

My parents have always been drinkers. Not like aaaalll day errrryday type of drinkers, just in social settings, wine with dinner and maybe a nip of whiskey before bed. I realize that the last one is definitely above "normal" levels for what's considered a "social drinker," but I also think it's more normal for their generation than mine.

As I got older, I knew my dad drank a lot. After getting divorced from my mom, then getting married to his mistress, and eventually divorcing her and marrying for the third time, the drinking only got worse. It was his method of coping.

The first time I knew my dad had a drinking problem was the first time he ended up in rehab. This seems like an *obvious* indicator that he had a problem drinking, however, the reason he was in rehab wasn't entirely his fault. His second wife was upset with him and she had a friend of hers write an anonymous letter to the clinic he had worked at for twenty-some years, telling them that he had a drinking problem and they needed to take action. They had no choice but to have him partake in a ninety-day inpatient rehab care.

Of course, this is the side of the story we were told, so of the legitimacy of it all, I'm not sure. He did his time and spent ninety days in that rehab facility, and I visited him there twice. The first time I visited Dad, I went alone. The facility was about an hour north of my house, and I was so nervous the entire drive there. What would it be like? Who would be there? Would it be scary? Would my dad be like my dad?

It wasn't scary, and my dad was my dad, but I sort of felt like I was visiting a teenager sent away to camp or someone at college. The campus of the facility seemed dorm-like, straight out of the 70s with boring brown brick walls, a communal bathroom with dingy cream tile, and shared rooms lining the halls. There was a commons area with mismatched couches and chairs, tables with board games and books scattered around the room, and a kitchen for snacks. There were men, the residents, roaming around and minding themselves with the occasional smile and "hello." It felt impolite to look too long or try to engage.

Dad and I took a walk outside where we could be alone and away from the dreary inside. Our conversation was light, discussing how Joey was doing (I only had one at the time), how work was, etc. Mostly I felt I was there to keep him company, which I could tell was much appreciated. I don't know how many visitors he had during his three months there, but I can hardly imagine how lonely he must've been. The second time I visited I brought Joey. We hung outside with my dad and the two of them ran around and played together, enjoying each other's company.

In the ninety days my dad spent in rehab, I don't think he learned a single thing. The facility follows the twelve steps of Alcoholics Anonymous, of which more than half are related to God and spirituality. But Dad was an atheist and did not find validity in this program. Even if you change "God" to "nature" or some other natural being, the program did not make sense to him.

Shortly after his stay in rehab, Dad and his second wife

divorced, and he got married for a third time. I don't really have many details during this time because it was around then that I was going through my divorce from Scott. I had never talked to Dad about my impending divorce, and rarely even saw him to catch up.

Dad and his new wife, Diane, got married in Vegas on his birthday, having a celebration for friends and family at home afterward. I showed up to the reception alone and immediately found my cousin, Grace, and asked her to grab a drink with me. She looked me up and down and said "You look great! Have you been working on this?", pointing to my rail-thin frame.

I'd lost so much weight from the stress of dealing with a cheating husband and beginning the divorce process, I was the smallest I'd been since being a varsity swimmer in high school. I shrugged a meek response, saying, "well... we're getting divorced, so I wouldn't say I've been 'working on it'," ending with a wink and a laugh.

She conveyed a myriad of emotions – shocked, happy, sad, confused – but relaxed when I said that I was ok with it and was happy to finally be on my own. Grace and her mom were the first in my extended family to know that anything had even been going on between Scott and me, not even my own dad knew. I wasn't about to ruin their wedding reception with the news, so I asked them to keep it hushed.

Dad and Diane moved to the cabin he had bought with my mom when I was in high school. This was the place he had always planned to retire, but he was nowhere near retirement yet. He had gotten a job at the Native American tribal clinic near the cabin, and it seemed to be his dream come true. However, once he moved there, we saw him less and less, usually only on Thanksgiving and Christmas.

About two years after their wedding celebration, which was also about two years since the boys and I had moved out on our own, I got a text from Diane on Black Friday, the day after they didn't show up for Thanksgiving. The excuse we were given was that they couldn't find boarding for the dogs, so they wouldn't be able to make it back to Minnesota. This was a common excuse, as they had three dogs, and I could imagine boarding them would be expensive.

It was a weekend that my boys were with Scott, my first Thanksgiving without them, and it was the first time I'd ever gone out shopping for Black Friday. I was wandering around the mall in town when Diane's text came through, disclosing,

"Ok, I need help. No more secrets. Your dad hasn't eaten in ten days and I can't get him up. He is suicidal. I'm calling 911 to get him to the hospital because he's too weak for me to get him into the car. Let family know. Time to get serious."

I didn't know what to do. They lived three and a half hours away and I didn't know where they would be taking him if she called 911. My body started shaking, unsure of what I should do first. She was his wife! The one in charge of caring for his well-being, and she just let me know that my dad was on the verge of death, via text.

I immediately tried calling her, but no answer. I called again. And again, three more times. I quickly learned that Diane was also an alcoholic and that she was in nearly as bad a shape as he was. Trying to communicate with her was absolutely maddening.

The ambulance brought Dad to a mental health facility nearly two hours away from their house, but it was one of the closest around. That night, as soon as we found out where he was being admitted, my youngest sister, Christine, and I hopped in the car and drove the hour and a half to the hospital. We arrived around 8:30 pm, only to be told that visiting hours are between 6-8 pm and we had missed the window. Thankfully, the doctor admitting him realized we were there and let us come see him since they were still working on getting him admitted.

Walking into the intake room, with stark-white walls and fluo-rescent lights screaming with light from the ceiling, I was surprised to see Dad sitting there. He was my dad, how he'd looked the last time I saw him, only more tired-looking and frail, draped with the hospital gown. I remember being surprised that he didn't look as bad as I thought. I had assumed he would be nearly unrecognizable given the text I'd gotten earlier this morning; *"he hasn't eaten or gotten out of bed in ten days. He's suicidal."*

Those things didn't sound like anything my dad would be capable of. He was a *doctor;* he knew how to take care of people. Yet, when was the last time I actually saw him? Christine and I sat down and Dad was happy to see us. He admitted that he had been struggling and drinking too much, but immediately went into doctor mode himself, going through his different blood and urine test results, assuring us that he was going to be just fine.

We didn't get to stay long as visiting hours were clearly over, so we said our goodbyes, gave hugs and said we would see him later. On the drive home, it was evident that Christine and I had a different opinion on how our dad was doing.

"He seemed pretty good to me, almost normal. I don't know what Diane was so worried about. He'll be just fine, I'm sure."

I knew that just because he seemed like himself didn't mean that he was just fine; an ambulance wouldn't make a two-hour trek to a mental health facility if they didn't think the issue was serious.

The next day, Saturday, we were told that my dad wouldn't be evaluated by a psychologist until Monday, and Diane understood this to mean that he was being released on Monday, which it certainly did not. The doctor called me to let me know that Diane was planning to come and pick Dad up early on Sunday instead, as Dad was insisting on checking himself out of the hospital.

I was not going to let this happen. I wanted the appointment with the psychologist to take place, and I knew if he left, he wouldn't go back. I was able to call and talk with Dad, begging him to stay just one more night. I pleaded with him, "Please do this one thing for me, simply because I'm asking you to."

To my surprise and relief, he agreed. I let out the breath I'd been holding in my chest and sighed an exhausted "Thank you," followed by "I love you," and then hung up.

Monday morning his body began to detox. He was so addicted to and full of, alcohol that it took his body over three days to be rid of what it was storing and to start craving more. The doctors called me on Monday to tell me that he would not be able to meet with the psychologist for a few days while he got through the worst of the detox. He was delusional and paranoid, hiding under his bed because of what he claimed he saw on the walls. He was suffering from alcohol withdrawal delirium, which is the most severe form of alcohol withdrawal. They gave him high doses of sedatives and anti-seizure medications just so that his body wouldn't shut down from the shock of the withdrawal.

Dad was in serious medical trouble and there was nothing I could do except talk with the doctors and nurses to help them make informed decisions about his care. I became his guardian and the one the medical staff contacted for updates and appointments. His wife was hysterical and complicated matters by not being sober herself. She thought she could go pick him up and they would go to rehab together, holding hands while walking the beach.

I went to visit Dad on Wednesday night, during visiting hours, three days after his detox truly began. Since the visiting hours wouldn't get me home until well after their bedtime, and they wouldn't be able to come with me, I brought my boys for an overnight at their in-home daycare. The drive alone would take over three hours, only to spend an hour or so with my dad. There was no way that Scott would be willing to take the boys for an unplanned night, nor did I want him to be a part of this personal situation.

Walking into the visiting room, which was also the intake room we'd been in the first time I came to visit, I did not recognize this man that was a new version of my father. He was not the same man I had seen only five days before. He was pale, gaunt, and grey. His eyes were black holes and staring, unable to focus on whatever was in their path. When I walked into the room, he began talking to me as if I were a nurse, while looking right at me.

I said, "Dad, it's me, Jessica."

He turned his face slightly, then looked down as if embarrassed, saying, "Oh, hey Jess. I thought you were a nurse!"

I was unsure if he actually recognized me then, or simply realized it was me by name only. He tried to converse with me, again going over his medical tests and blood counts, none of it making any sense to me. I avoided looking directly at him for fear that my tears would burst out of the dam I'd been trying so hard to keep them behind. He eventually started talking about some of the other patients, explaining their diagnoses to me as if he were their doctor, and I could start to see a glimpse of the man I knew as my dad peeking through.

We sat in stillness for a little while longer until I said I best be going. We didn't know what lay ahead or how long he would need to remain in the hospital, so for now we just hugged and said our goodbyes.

I held it together just barely long enough to make it to the parking lot. It was cold and the street was icy, and I managed to step over snowbanks and dodge the icy spots through the pools of tears filling my eyes. The dams burst and the tears rushed down my cheeks; my throat broke out in sobs as I wondered what was going to happen with him. What would come next? My dark and lonely drive home was spotted with tears and I don't think I stopped crying for the rest of the night. I was so grateful that the boys were in the care of someone else and I could cry myself to sleep, alone in the dark.

The next day, Thursday, I received a text from Diane saying that my dad was planning to escape the hospital on Friday if they didn't let him out. She said she was worried because he didn't have his wallet and she didn't know how he'd get home.

Immediately, I called the social worker and let them know that my dad seemed to be planning an escape. They assured me that he would not be able to just up and leave, foiling his plot to flee. It kinda made me giggle thinking about it: my dad sneaking out of the heavy, electronically monitored door in his hospital gown, no shoes, no wallet, trying to flag down a taxi. But then it also makes me sad, because this is an exact scene from a movie of someone escaping a mental hospital. And that was the situation we were in; my dad was plotting his escape from a mental hospital...

Later that afternoon, the social worker called me and asked if we'd be able to come in for a family meeting the next morning and that they were planning to release my dad. There was no reason they could hold him any longer now that he was past the potentially fatal detox period.

The meeting was set for Friday morning, and I took the day off work. Dad's brother and one of my aunts planned to attend the meeting with me, as did Diane. The four of us sat there with my dad and his medical team discussing what would happen next. The doctors and specialists assured us and him that he would not be ready to go back to his same old life, that he should not go immediately back to his house, but rather an inpatient rehab facility.

He refused. And with his refusal, so came his wife's refusal. The doctors told him that if he ever drank again, even one drink, he could likely die. I cried; mean, angry tears that screamed "I do not agree with this." I begged that he come live with me and I would take care of him. My aunt pleaded with him that I was the one needing caretaking as I was a single mom to young boys and had recently gone through a horrible divorce. That *he* should be the one taking care of *me,* yet here we were, witnessing his refusal to let me take care of *him.*

We each looked at the doctors with eyes begging them to tell us what to do, how we could make this ok. But there was nothing they could do; my dad was able to make his own decisions and he had said a stubborn "no" to any offer of help. I was furious and felt lost, hopeless, and hurt. Here I was, visiting my dad in the hospital hours away from my house for the third time in a week, which was more than I'd seen him in the last year and a half, begging him to get help; to let me, us, help him. The answer was simply, no.

I walked out of the meeting room without even saying goodbye to my dad. I just couldn't face the fact that he wanted to go right back into the situation that had brought him to this hospital. My aunt and uncle were shortly by my side in the parking lot, with Diane not far behind. She had packed up all the booze they had in the house and brought it for us to take. That was their plan, give away the alcohol and we'll be alright.

My uncle took the box of liquor bottles and put it in his trunk while Diane went back inside to be with my dad. I cried out of frustration and sadness and hugged my aunt and uncle goodbye. We all felt defeated and hopeless.

Three weeks later I received an envelope from my dad. The only thing in it was a printed piece of paper with his blood work and medical test results on it, showing that he was following up with a local clinic and maintaining his recently found sobriety. I texted him to thank him for sending it and that I hoped he was feeling alright. Again, our routine went back to seeing each other only at holidays and texting occasionally.

He began drinking again shortly after, losing his job, and ending up back in the hospital. I truly didn't think he'd make it through after the previous doctors had said "even one more drink could kill you." It hadn't been a scare tactic; it was the truth from their perspective. I believed it and I have been terrified that that deadly drink will someday come.

Through all of this, he's still my dad and I love and care about him, and I know he cares for us too. But since I've been let down so many times, by him but also by Scott, I've made a conscious choice to minimize the amount I can give of myself to others with nothing in return. I know that he has a disease, and I don't blame him; I just know I can't give any more of myself to him. I wish I could have done more to help, but he didn't want it. You can't help someone until they're willing to accept help, and I have relied on that motto to get me through.

I Want to Have Your Baby

When David was about three, nearly two years post-separation from my Scott, I decided I wanted to explore surrogacy. I was in my mid-thirties, not ready to begin dating, and not sure if I would ever meet someone with whom to have any more children of my own. I was not ready to be done with the experience of seeing the two pink lines, or the feeling of growing a life inside me, but I was also confident that I was not ready for another child. In case I never got the chance to have another of my own, I wanted to at least offer that to another family.

Even before I had children of my own, I was fascinated by pregnancy and childbirth. I always knew in my heart that if one of my sisters ever needed me to carry their baby, I would do so without a second thought. The cousins on my mom's side were all older than me. Growing up, I learned that one of those cousins donated her eggs to her sister so that, after surviving ovarian cancer, she could have two children of her own. I always admired this effort, on both sides; one for being thoughtful enough to ask for help from her sister and the other for being caring enough to offer her eggs.

Surrogacy is not taken lightly. I signed up with a local agency and began the process to see if I would be qualified. There were several intake phone interviews, a lot of paperwork and doctor's visits, and a lengthy session with a psychologist. I hadn't seen a psychologist since I had ghosted the last one, and my session didn't seem complete unless I shared the details of the tumultuousness of the divorce. I told it all, holding back tears where I could, but was honest.

When I was done sharing, I thought she would tell me that I was not fit to pursue surrogacy, since I had gone through so much. Would she think I wasn't emotionally available to still be a good mother to my children while being exhausted from growing someone else's child? Did she think I'd be mentally stable enough to hand over the baby at the end? I asked her those questions, to be sure I had all the answers. She assured me that she knew I was a perfect candidate and that what I was doing was brave.

I didn't tell anyone that I was taking this path. I suppose it was a learned behavior from being with Scott; I didn't tell because I didn't want to be judged. The same applied to my decision to become a surrogate. This was something I wanted to do for myself and I didn't want anyone to try to talk me out of it. I was on my own and able to make my own decisions and did not want to be influenced. For some reason, I assumed people would tell me not to do it, that I wasn't capable of such a big thing all on my own.

This was when I found out that Scott had access to my email. I was sitting at home one night when Mom called to tell me she'd heard something and needed to discuss it with me.

"Hi honey," she said, "I just got off the phone with Scott."

My jaw dropped, questioning, "What in the hell did he want?"

She said that Scott called her out of the blue and proceeded to tell her about my "scandalous" behavior, wanting to become a surrogate. He thought that it wasn't appropriate for a single mom to be out trying to have other people's children and wanted to make sure my mom knew what I was up to.

Of course, she didn't, because I hadn't told anyone about it. His behavior was exactly why I hadn't. It was his voice inside my head all along, telling me that I wasn't good enough to do something like this and that it was a "scandalous" thing to do rather than something helpful out of love and compassion.

"Is any of it true? Are you wanting to be a surrogate?" she asked, mostly assuming that he had come up with some lie to stir up drama.

I felt like I was in trouble, both for trying to become a surrogate and also for hiding it.

I came clean and told her the details. "Yes, I've been working with an agency, getting all the necessary doctor's visits and paperwork completed before we work on finding a match."

"Wow! Are you sure this is something you're up for?" she asked, followed by the standard question everyone has about surrogacy, "Are you going to be able to give the baby up at the end?" She wasn't telling me I wasn't capable, but she knew it was a big undertaking.

The thing about surrogacy is that you go into it knowing you're having someone else's child. You don't suddenly find yourself pregnant, deciding whether to give it up for adoption. The baby *wouldn't* be mine to keep, but I understand the question, I really do. Of course, it would be hard not to be attached, to go home without a baby in your arms at the end. But the point of surrogacy is that you're giving someone else the child they've longed for, helping them fulfill their dreams. That is the blessing after carrying a child for nine months.

My mom understood that Scott was not to be taken seriously and that I was free to do what I pleased, but I'm not sure she quite understood my desire to become a surrogate. She was supportive regardless, and we finished the call with her assuring me that she was proud of me, and me realizing I needed to change all of my passwords, immediately.

Once I was approved to become a surrogate with the agency, I was ready to be matched with prospective parents. Honestly, I had never given any thought to the matching process, and I panicked! The agency sent me a bio for a couple looking for a surrogate, and I suddenly found myself questioning my worth. Will they think I'm capable of taking care of their growing baby while I was so busy taking care of my own? I'm a single mom with little help, is this too much?

It took me a long time to realize that the couple was trying to "woo" *me* and not the other way around. Here I thought I needed to prove myself, prove that I would be a good foster womb for their child when there are far more couples in contention than surrogates available. *They* wanted to be *chosen* to begin their next journey to become parents, and they were thrilled that I was willing.

We set up a phone interview to get to know each other a little, and the anticipation was far worse than a job interview or first date. We were going to determine if we were a good fit to try and bring a child into the world together. Complete strangers, skipping the dating period and marriage, going straight for the baby carriage.

Alice and Matt were a wonderful, wealthy couple from Canada, and had been trying everything under the Eastern and Western medicinal suns to get pregnant with no such luck. I don't know why I was surprised at how much we had in common and how quickly they felt like a part of my family. Alice and I got along seamlessly from the start. I was so excited to share this experience together!

They had frozen embryos in Toronto and we planned to do the embryo transfer within three months, so I had to begin medication to suppress my cycle right away. During my agency interviews, they often asked if I had any questions, which I rarely did. I had no idea how little I knew about becoming a surrogate, so I didn't know what questions to ask. I was notified that I would be receiving my medication in the mail and that there were videos I could watch on how to self-administer my daily shots. It was assumed that I would likely have someone living with me that could assist in providing my shots, which was not the case.

Once the medication arrived, I started watching the videos on how to pinch the fat on my stomach, insert the needle into said fat and dispense the liquid into myself. I have never been able to watch the processes of having my blood drawn or a nurse delivering a shot, and there I was, needing to not only watch but having to put the needle in myself. I opened the package with the first needle and said, out loud, "Oh, thank god!" when I saw a teeny tiny little needle. It was about two inches long and the diameter of a very small sewing needle. Even still, I wasn't sure that I'd be able to do it.

I watched the video over and over, hoping that I would draw encouragement from it. It must've worked because I finally decided to give it a try. I pulled the medicine into the syringe as instructed and set the readied needle to rest on the counter while I used the alcohol wipe to clean and prep the area. I cleaned a nice large surface area, just in case my needle stab wasn't too accurate.

Then I gathered the pinch of fat in between the thumb and index finger of my left hand and picked up the syringe in my right hand with my pointer finger lightly resting on the plunger end, ready to administer. Then I realized I needed to get the needle into the fat before I could slide the plunger in, so I removed my finger from the trigger. I held the syringe with my thumb and first two fingers and breathed in slowly. I practiced aiming slowly, about five to six times before I decided I had to just do it and get it over with.

I counted to myself, "one... two... sigh... *three"* and pulled my hand toward my wad of fat, the needle sliding nearly effortlessly into my skin. It was in! I couldn't believe it was that easy and nearly painless. I finally put my finger on the end of the plunger and pushed the medicine in; I couldn't even feel it. After that, it was much easier, as most things are once you learn they aren't as horrible as you imagined.

The embryo transfer was scheduled about a month out, which was to take place in Canada, just three months after first meeting Alice and Matt. Thankfully, I already had a valid passport, and it was scheduled on a weekend when my boys were with Scott. It couldn't have worked out better.

I had to give myself daily shots at certain, specific times of the day. Once I met my friend for a drink after work on a Friday night. We met at the restaurant and she slipped into the passenger seat of my car in the parking lot, waiting for me to give myself a shot. It was routine by then, so a quick, two-minute process before we headed in. It was a Friday night around dinner time, but they were expecting a band so they ID'd us at the door to make sure we were of drinking age. It was quite comical, going from administering myself medication to try to help another couple have a family, to being carded at the door of a bar.

Finally, the time came for me to fly to Canada to meet Alice and Matt in person. I was allowed to bring a support person, which is typically a spouse, and I chose my closest friend, Harper. It felt like a girlfriend's getaway, except that it wasn't, not even in the slightest. The whole trip there I kept thinking, "Hopefully I come back pregnant!" My hopes were so high that I didn't even see an alternative. I just knew I would be carrying their baby home, even though I'd still have days to wait to find out if I was, actually pregnant.

Toronto is very much like San Francisco, and even though I'd never been there before, it felt familiar, like I was on a work trip. The front desk host at the hotel, making small talk, asked "What brings you to Toronto?"

Not wanting to get into the details or offer too much personal information, instead of saying "I'm here to transfer an embryo in the hopes of becoming a surrogate!" I simply stated "Work." And that was that; an uncomplicated exchange of niceties between two strangers that will never know anything more of the other.

Alice and Matt picked Harper and me up for dinner, which was to be our first meeting on our journey of trying to expand their family. We were all so thrilled to be meeting and enjoyed lighthearted conversation over dinner. They took us to a fancy restaurant that surely required reservations. Not so fancy that it required a little black dress, but the food was posh and most certainly, delicious! We all celebrated with a drink, assuming that it would be my last for a while. It was a short dinner as it was getting late and we were tired from traveling. Afterward, they brought us back to the hotel to rest, for in the morning we would be on our way to the clinic.

A bundle of nerves and excitement, I wasn't quite ready to sleep, so we decided to set up a movie on Netflix. Harper ingeniously brought all the right cable hook-ups to get her iPad connected to the TV, just to discover that we only had access to Canadian Netflix and our available choices were limited. We settled on some comedy and chatted throughout it, impatient for the morning to arrive.

With coffees in hand, we finally got to the clinic to do what we came here to do. Alice checked us in, and I could tell she'd been here before. Her journey to this point had been a long one, and she had tried to get pregnant for years. As someone that got pregnant the first time both times I tried, I cannot relate to her nor understand what she has gone through, not even in the slightest. Yet, I wished to help her have a child of her own, the greatest gift I had to offer her.

The four of us, Harper, Alice, Matt, and I all sat together in the waiting room until it was our turn to meet with the doctor. I looked around the room, seeing other couples patiently awaiting their turn as well, wondering where along their journey they were. How many times had they found themselves back here? What must it feel like to be waiting to find out whether you have enough viable embryos, or whether your egg or sperm count is sufficient? A nurse came and called us back, but only three of us followed the nurse, leaving Harper to pass the time alone in the waiting room chair.

We walked down the hallway to the doctor's office, meeting him behind his large wooden desk where he stood up just enough to shake Matt and Alice's hands before sitting again. Alice and I sat at the two chairs in front of his desk while Matt stood behind us, awaiting the status of the embryo availability for that day's transfer. There were only two viable embryos, and it was decided that we would only transfer one this time, saving the second for another try.

I was new to this conversation and not particularly part of the discussion as the doctor informed them that, while the embryo was "grade A" (the best), there was a small percent chance that it would take; small as in a one to three percent chance. Again, this information wasn't necessarily presented *to* me, but rather peripherally, and I was left questioning the info I had overheard.

"A one to three percent chance it will take?" I thought. "That doesn't seem very likely."

But Matt and Alice nodded their heads that they understood and that, while small, there was still a good chance with this grade A embryo.

"Let's do this!" they all agreed, and we all stood up to move into a separate room where we would do the transfer.

The room looked very much like any regular visit to your OB or gyno's clinic. There was an exam table along the side, with a counter, sink and storage cabinets along the other wall. The only real difference was a stainless-steel door in the wall next to the exam table, similar to the door in the bathroom where you would pass your "cup o' pee" through. This small door was for the doctor to receive the embryo just before transferring it into my uterus.

The nurse handed me a paper sheet and asked me to get undressed from the waist down, while they waited in the hall. Once they left and I was undressed, I sat on the end of the table with the sheet across my lap. This was certainly not a standard visit to my gyno! What would happen when they came back in? Would they watch the doctor down there while my legs were spread? I was suddenly incredibly nervous about all of the unknowns of this procedure.

Matt and Alice came back in with the nurse, but they immediately went up near my head. Matt stood toward the back of the room while Alice stood right next to me, wanting to be every bit a part of the action. The doctor followed shortly and set up camp by my legs, propping them up in the stirrups. There wasn't much time spent waiting around here, and he got right to business. He took the equipment from the nurse on the other side of the little door in the wall, describing what he would be doing. There was a large syringe with a long catheter attached to it that he would thread through my cervix, finding the perfect spot to place the embryo in my uterus by using ultrasound.

The whole procedure only took minutes and soon, everyone was back in the hall, waiting for me to get dressed. I had laid on the table for the required ten minutes before standing to put my pants on, and I was terrified. They were counting on *me* for this embryo to stick! *Why would they let me just walk around this soon after? Shouldn't I lie around with my feet up for days until we know it worked?* Apparently not. They all assured me that this was standard procedure and that I was more than ok to go back to my hotel room and watch movies the rest of the day.

Our flight back home was the following morning, and I was nothing but optimistic that I would soon find out we were pregnant. I waited a few days before I started peeing on a stick, hoping to see the sign that the transfer had been successful. Alice didn't want me to give her any info at all, preferring to wait until we had the blood test after about two weeks. Every morning and every night I took a pregnancy test, squinting and using varying levels of light to read it with, sometimes tricking myself that it was positive. It never was, and neither was the official blood test. Another of many letdowns for Alice, but a major first for me.

I was ready to try again right away. "I'm ready when you are!" I told Alice, indicating that I'd be available to fly to Toronto the following month. She wasn't as eager. She needed time to process another loss, accepting that she only had one more try at this, and she asked that we give it a couple more months before trying again. It was then that I realized the magnitude of this process. Yes, I was naively hopeful that this would work as I'd gotten pregnant so easily before, but this wasn't about me and my ability to become pregnant, not really. This was a part of her and Matt, and they only had a *one to three percent* chance that it would work. And this was their last chance.

After waiting three months, the time had come for us to try the transfer again. This time, I went alone, as the agency only paid for a companion for the first trip. I knew what to expect this time and I was aware of the routine. We found ourselves back at the clinic in the morning, following the same process as the first, except this time I said a little prayer after the doctor transferred the embryo and the crew waited in the hall while I got dressed. I placed my hand on my stomach and prayed to the universe to *please* let this one take, for Alice.

The next day I was on a plane back home again, this time much more nervous than hopeful. "This has to work!" I thought, telling myself over and over that this time, it would.

This time I waited longer to start taking the pregnancy tests. I was so very hopeful, but also incredibly nervous. One morning's test presented the faintest line you ever did see.

"Eeeeeek!" I became giddy with happiness, knowing that this time was it. Except, it wasn't. Every test I took from then on was negative, including the official blood test. It hadn't worked, and I was not pregnant. I apologized over and over to Alice, telling her how sorry I was that we were not going to be having a baby.

I felt like it was my fault, that I had failed her. But I realized that she didn't blame me at all. She knew what her odds were, and while she wanted this to work more than anything in the world, she was realistic and understood that it just wasn't meant to be. My apologizing made her try to make *me* feel better when all she wanted to do was mourn the loss of the chance of having a child of her own. I stopped apologizing and started thanking her for allowing me to have the opportunity to try and do this for her.

Alice and I stayed in contact for a while after, but I think I might have been just a reminder of a piece of her life she had to let go of. A few months passed and I sent her a gift, to let her know I was thinking about her, and to recognize what we'd gone through together. It was a long necklace chain with a sterling silver bird's nest containing three bird's eggs at the end, symbolizing the two embryos we'd tried and all that she'd tried before we met. I will never understand her loss and the grief she must carry, but I'm so thankful for the opportunity to have experienced the process with her.

Dating, Again

On one of my work trips to San Francisco, I had a layover in Portland. I was standing near the gate with still an hour left until boarding. There were two gates full of people waiting, so when a man was standing nearly next to me, I hardly noticed until he started chatting with me, asking, "Are you waiting for the Chicago flight?"

I replied, "Oh, no, I'm over here," pointing to the opposite gate, "waiting to go to San Francisco."

He was an average guy, probably in his forties, five foot ten inches, bald, and a little stocky. He was friendly and seemed to want to pass the time.

"I live in the bay area," he said. Then, "I just came from there on my way to Chicago."

I am not big into small talk chit-chat, so I only replied out of politeness, "I'm on my way there for work. I work in operations for a software company."

Turned out, he also worked in the software industry, which made sense since he lived in the bay area. We stood there in silence for a few moments when he asked, "Do you have a business card?"

I laughed and felt my cheeks turn pink, my gaze drifting toward the floor. I responded, "No, I'm not important enough for those!" and laughed again.

"Well, here's mine then, ok?" he said as he handed me the little white card with his name and contact info on it. I thanked him for the card and was also very thankful that his flight was starting to board. We said goodbye and he walked over to his gate.

I was pretty confused by the exchange, wondering what had just happened. Why did he give me his card? Is that what business travelers do when they find others in the same industry? I looked down at his business card and saw that he was a "C-Level" boss at an extremely large tech company. Why would someone so high up be interested in my contact info? Did he want to offer me a job?

Once aboard the plane, I started messaging with one of my co-workers, telling him what happened and looking for guidance.

"He was totally into you," he wrote, "message him and find out!"

So, I did, I pulled up an email and typed a short and sweet message.

"Hey!

It was nice meeting you today. I hope your flight made it safely.

Best,

Jessica."

Almost instantly I got a message back:

"Hi, Jessica,

It was very nice meeting you, too. I will be back in the bay area in a few days if you'd have a free night to get dinner or a drink.

Best,

Alex"

Wow, so he really *was* interested in me. Huh. At least my looks, anyway, because he couldn't possibly have gotten to know anything about me in the five minutes we chatted... But I was intrigued, and was out of town, away from my responsibilities at home, so I thought, *why not?* We agreed to meet for a drink after my team's dinner event on Wednesday night.

Alex and I enjoyed each other's company for some drinks at the bar before walking the cobblestone streets outside. He was kind and charming and we found a lot to talk about. My divorce wasn't finalized yet, so we talked a bit about that and how he'd never been married.

He asked if I wanted to go for a drive to see his place. Again, not being responsible for anything else felt wonderful and again I thought, *Why not?*

The work friend I had been messaging on the plane knew about this late-night plan for drinks and I knew he would be waiting up to make sure I got back to the hotel safely, so I messaged him to let him know that I would be out for a while. He was worried about me, but we both knew who this guy was after Googling him, realizing he was who he said he was and figured it seemed harmless.

By the time we got to his condo, I was definitely feeling the drinks I'd had throughout the evening. We rode the elevator up to the tenth floor, and I was surprised at how average the whole place was. It seemed like any single guy's bachelor pad, and I figured he just must travel so often that he doesn't need anything too fancy. I appreciated the humbleness of the place.

I sat down on the black leather couch in the living room, while he brought me a glass of wine. He set it on the wooden coffee table, which he described as something he'd made himself. It was quite impressive craftsmanship! I looked around the one-bedroom condo, noticing how bare everything seemed, almost like he had just moved in. It felt very transitional or temporary.

Eventually, we made our way into the bedroom, because of course, why else had he brought me there? The sex was terrible and fast, and we essentially banged it out and got dressed again to bring me back to the hotel. I expected this to be a one-night stand and that I would never hear from him again, but I was wrong.

Over the following weeks, he'd call me out of the blue and we'd text here and there. I tried so hard to find out what I could about him, stalking his online presence, but I found nothing about his personal life at all. His almost nerdy demeanor felt endearing and refreshing like he was truly just a nice guy that wasn't used to dating.

Alex told me he had a layover in Minneapolis and wanted to meet for dinner. We set it up so that I would pick him up at his hotel and we'd have dinner nearby. This time, the conversation felt more forced and awkward, and it wasn't as engaging as the first time we'd been together. I had made reservations for a fancy Italian restaurant that we often held lunch meetings at for work. It was a warm summer evening and we sat on the patio in the shade. Alex was sweating and seemed more uncomfortable than he should've been, but maybe he just wasn't used to the humidity.

After dinner, I drove him back to his hotel and again agreed to come up to his room. On the elevator ride, he started kissing my neck and telling me how much he liked my white pants. By the time we got to his room, I decided I was not going to have sex with him. The first time was awful, and the connection we may have had was gone. I said, "I have my period, so we can't have sex."

He was annoyed, and asked, "Who wears white pants when they have their period?"

"I do!" I responded with an annoyed smile.

We made our way to his hotel room, and once inside I walked over to the window to check out the view, but it was only of the parking lot and highway beyond. He walked up behind me, put his arms around me, and said, "I was hoping we could make this official."

I turned around to face him. "What do you mean?" I asked.

"I like you, and I want us to be in a committed relationship." He replied.

Say what now? Where was this coming from? I stammered, "I

don't think that's going to happen. You travel all the time for work, and I can't just move to San Francisco. I don't see how we would ever see each other."

He tried to tell me that he enjoyed spending time with me and that he saw a future for us.

"I'm sorry, but that is just not going to happen." I mustered before giving him one last hug goodbye. I thanked him for dinner and made my way to the door. He didn't walk me to my car, which I was grateful for, but once I got to my car I looked up and saw him watching me from his hotel window. I waved, and he waved back, and that was the last time I saw him.

Occasionally, I would think about him, Googling his name to see what new info I could find. My searching skills got more refined and I ended up finding out that he had a wife, who happened to look a whole lot like me, and two kids barely older than my own. I felt awful, knowing that I was likely not the only woman to be duped by him, wondering how many airport pickups there'd been throughout their marriage. I wondered if she knew and allowed it, as I had, or was completely in the dark about it all.

Did she know about his condo that he'd taken me to? At least now it made sense for why it felt like a temporary bachelor pad. How many women had he brought there? I'm thankful that we had only seen each other twice, the second time being to say goodbye, and also that I didn't get wrapped up in something that was destined for tragedy.

For about three years after getting divorced, my life was a series of getting through the days. But eventually, I decided I was ready to try to find companionship. Scott was complying with the every-other-weekend schedule, so the boys were consistently gone every other weekend, and I could find some time to plan to do other things. I didn't have many friends, other than some girls at work, and I wasn't going out or brunching on the weekends where I might meet someone, so I decided I would try online dating.

I was terrified of the idea because I had no clue what I was looking for or even really what I would say in my profile. "Single mom of two young kids." That was about how I defined my life at the time. I did nothing except work and take care of my boys, no hobbies, no free time whatsoever. Clearly, that wasn't going to land me any dates, so I had to do my research.

I signed up for a couple of the popular free dating apps, both as a male and a female, and started looking at profiles. What were guys looking for? What were they putting on their profiles? What were the girls saying about themselves? I didn't set anything up for my profile, so I knew I wasn't going to get any quality prospects, but I wanted to know what was out there so that I had even an ounce of a clue where to start with my real profile. How would I compare? Ugh, if you have never tried online dating, it is complicated and incredibly scary to put yourself out there for anyone to critique, without you ever knowing they even visited your profile.

Once I had my profile active, I started getting messages from guys. Sitting there, reading through their notes and profiles, I suddenly threw my phone down. Nope, I can't do this. I am NOT ready for this. I don't even know what to *say* to them! Who am I without explaining all the baggage I carry? I haven't been "me" in years, and I have no idea what is even remotely interesting about myself. I can't do it and I delete the apps.

After a few days of thinking constantly about this whole new world of instantly available men, I decided I needed to at least try it again. I got everything back up and running and convinced myself to just read the messages and look at profiles. Nothing was forcing me to respond to any of them, and upon realizing this, I was able to take it all in without the pressure of actually talking to anyone.

It took weeks for me to feel comfortable enough to respond to a few guys. I started simply with niceties and easy small talk, but then shiz got real when date requests came in. Again, I panicked. *I'm not available for two weeks from now! Can he wait that long? Is my schedule too rigid and complicated?* I decided that all I could do was try.

Sometimes I'd get pushback like "Can't you find a sitter?" or even just a non-reply, but in general, I found that most guys were very accommodating and just fine waiting until I would be free.

The first several dates were *hard*. I met my now ex-husband at nineteen and had never actually *dated* in my adult life. I was comfortable talking to guys; it had always been easier for me to talk to guys over girls, so that wasn't the problem. The problem was that I didn't know how to talk about *myself*. Again, I felt like I had nothing to share outside of talking about my kids, and who wants to do that on a first date?

Eventually, I made myself sit down and write out the things I liked to do so that it became more natural for me to recall them. *I love food, but I'm not going to call myself a "foodie", because what does that even mean other than "I'm a food snob." I love to travel, but for the foreseeable next ten years or more it will have to be a quick weekend getaway because I have no one to watch my kids. Probably should skip that one...*

I like to grocery shop and aimlessly walk around the shopping mall. Again, not too intriguing. People always seem to have hobbies, like biking or running, knitting or cooking, etc. But not me. When my kids were away, I'd spend time cleaning or binge-watching movies. So, I guess, there you have it – my hobbies included watching tv, marathon style, and de-kidifying my house.

Dating got easier after the first couple of dates, and it ended up being kind of fun. I was the center of the office gossip and everyone would stop by early in the week to hear how the latest date went, and on Thursday/Fridays to see what I may have lined up for the weekend. I think we all had a blast via my newly discovered social life.

I dated some pretty interesting men that year. There was the guy who lived alone, having his two boys half the time, except his place looked like a frat house and he kept the Christmas tree up year 'round. He was sure he wanted more kids, even though he'd had a vasectomy years ago.

There was the corporate attorney who was charming, in a way, simply because he seemed to be learning how to be charming. On the second or third date, he told me a fun fact about himself, which was that he had lost nearly 200 pounds over the last couple of years. I was astounded because that was a major accomplishment and something you would simply have to take pride in! His attitude made more sense after that announcement because it was previously hard to place his mildly cocky demeanor. He was sweet but had an edge to him, almost like he was playing hard-to-get.

We had gone on a few dates when Mother's Day came around. Most days, we texted back and forth occasionally throughout the day, but it was almost into the evening on Mother's Day when I hadn't heard a word from him. I finally got a text from him around dinner simply saying, "What's up?"

While he'd never been married nor had any kids of his own, I expected some acknowledgment of the holiday for me, if he cared about me at all. I texted back "Not much, just another day." Because Mother's Day is just another day when you're a single mom of young kids. That was the last of our communication.

Another date was the guy that started the date by telling me he had a nervous habit of playing with a tube of Chapstick, for which he did for the entirety of the date. The waitress came by at one point to pick up my purse from the floor, saying "It's bad luck to leave your purse on the floor!" and winked at me. It must've been obvious that this was a first date, exuding awkwardness, and we never spoke again.

There was the guy that wanted to find true love on a first date. He spent the entire date interviewing me to see if I would be a good wife and mom. While it wasn't as awkward or uncomfortable as it sounds, it certainly wasn't a match. He walked me to my car in the underground parking garage, which I was thankful for, until he unexpectedly kissed me with some dramatic passion that I was not aware he had for me. We did not talk again after that date.

Some of the dates were one date only, a few of them became multiple dates, and a couple resulted in more serious relationships. But through all of them, I still felt like they were missing something. Here I was, finally in a position to *choose* a partner, but I really couldn't place what it was that I wanted or what I was missing. I got incredibly good at reading between the lines in their dating profiles, studying their picture choices, and determining that most men were either avid hunters/fishermen, or they had a huge group of brosefs and likely spent a lot of time going out with their buddies. I was not interested in someone that would be gone often; that part I did know. I wanted a companion and someone to share the daily routine with.

I met Ben on eHarmony, becoming serious pretty quickly. He was a chef and had just started a new healthy cooking program at a local hospital. He loved his career and loved food even more than I did. He lived alone with his small pup in a neighborhood where people could ride their bikes to Uptown or around the local lakes. His house was updated and clean, and he had fancy towels and bedding. I stayed over on the weekends during which I didn't have the boys, and he'd bring me coffee in bed along with some breakfast he'd whipped up. I had never been so pampered by a guy before.

We spent our time together going out to dinner, watching movies, or riding our bikes around the lakes. Eventually, I introduced him to my boys, and they became fast friends. They'd play board games together or play with the dog, and they all got along great. His parents lived in a small town in a big cabin on a lake a few hours from our house. We took the boys there a couple of times, enjoying the fourth of July out on the boat and riding the four-wheelers around the local dirt roads.

I thoroughly enjoyed spending time with Ben, and after a couple of months, we started talking about what it would look like if we became serious. The boys and I lived in a suburb about thirty minutes out of the city, and he loved living near the city, not sure he'd be able to make the move to suburbia. Since we didn't need to make any decisions any time soon, we continued on, seeing each other on the weekends when we could.

While the day-to-day stuff with Ben was wonderful - who wouldn't love fancy food and breakfast in bed? - there was a glaring issue that seemed to never quite be addressed; we had never had sex. This wasn't an agreed-upon thing like we were waiting for the appropriate amount of time, this was something I realized was actually a problem for him; he wasn't able to get an erection. We tried, maybe twice, but it just wouldn't work. He would get frustrated and say that he should probably see a doctor, but he'd never make an appointment. I didn't push the issue, because to be honest, I was fine being with a man where sex wasn't everything, and he liked to take care of me!

One morning after he'd left for work, I found a box in the bathroom garbage of some "Chinese Viagra" or something he'd bought off the internet. We hadn't tried to have sex recently, so I wondered if he'd tried it while alone, realizing it didn't work. I never asked him about it, but I was frustrated that at forty-some years old that he'd rather try something off the internet rather than talk to a doctor about it. Did he not *want* to have sex?

I went back to the posh, plush bed to watch some TV before getting dressed and going on with my day. I couldn't get the internet-drugs out of my mind and decided to snoop in his nightstand. I opened the drawer, which was neatly organized, and found two movie stubs sitting right there on the top. I picked them up, thinking how cute it was that he saved them from when we went to the movies. Except, it wasn't a movie I'd seen.

Confused, I checked the date, thinking it must've been from before we met. It wasn't; it had been from about two weeks before, and immediately my stomach started doing flip-flops. I could feel it fill with acid and my whole body got hot. I sat up; my face scrunched into a "what the hell is happening?" contortion and I jumped out of bed, pacing the floor.

"What was two weeks ago?" I asked myself. "When did he go to a movie? And with whom?" My mind was racing, and I couldn't figure it out. This wasn't about him going to a movie without me, it was that he didn't tell me about it, and he felt the need to keep the ticket stubs. I put them back in the drawer and pulled up our texts, scrolling up to the date printed on the tickets.

"I'm heading off to bed early. Night!" was the text I got that day at 9:51 pm. The movie was to start at 10:25 pm. He flat-out *lied* to me. This was the exact opposite situation that I was in with Scott the night I found the texts from Vegas girl. He told her he was going to bed while he was at home with me, while Ben told me he was going to bed while with someone else!

I had to get out of there! I grabbed my things and jumped into the car, calling my friend Harper as soon as I backed out of the driveway. I told her what had happened, about the imitation Viagra, the movie tickets, and the lie. Normally, the discussion would be "boy, BYE!" and she'd tell me to never talk to him again. However, she knew how good things had been between us, and that he truly seemed to be a nice guy. She convinced me that I needed to confront him about it and see what his reaction would be. I agreed and decided I would meet him back at his house after he was done with work.

Once at his house, face to face with him, I felt powerful for the first time. I knew that I deserved the truth and that I deserved an apology for being lied to. I decided that I only really cared about the deceit of the movie tickets and the "early to bed" text, so that is what I confronted him with.

"I saw movie ticket stubs on your nightstand and when I looked at them, I realized it was not a movie we saw together." He became nervous, and I could tell he was trying to see how he could get his way out of it.

"I'm sorry," he choked, his voice crackly with nerves. "I went to that movie with a friend, and I'm sorry I lied about it."

I wasn't used to apologies, and while I still didn't have a good explanation or excuse, I believed that he was sorry, for what though, I wasn't sure. He wouldn't offer any more information, and I didn't feel like pressing the issue. I knew a few of his friends, but it hadn't been with one of them or he would've mentioned it. Since we weren't having any sex, I wasn't even worried that he was cheating on me or seeing someone else, even though the like-lihood was pretty high, given the situation.

We let it go and found a movie to watch on T.V. By 9 pm, he was sleeping next to me on the couch, so I continued to watch the movie myself. When it was over, I got up and started putting on my coat and shoes, until he woke up.

"Where are you going?" he asked, groggily.

"I'm just going to go home tonight," I responded. "You're tired and I was just going to let you rest."

"Don't go!" he protested, "Let's go up to bed together."

I was irritated but decided that it was easier to crawl into bed there rather than drive the thirty minutes home. Once in bed though, I was uncomfortable. There was an elephant in the room, and I couldn't fall asleep. I tossed and turned while he passed out instantly. Why was he so tired? He always seemed tired. I had caught him in a lie about going to bed early when he really went to a late-night movie; was he doing this often? Was this just what happened to men in their forties when they worked a lot? Maybe there was something medical going on, but we wouldn't know since he wouldn't even see a doctor for his impotence...

I left the next morning, after my coffee in bed, and we didn't see each other until two weekends later. We had decided on dinner at the restaurant down the street, first discussing walking there, but realized we'd rather just drive. We sat down and ordered our drinks, spending the time chatting about our days until the drinks came, and we ordered our food.

As soon as the server left with our order, Ben said, "I don't think we should see each other anymore."

I was mid-sip of my beer, staring at him from over the end of my glass.

Not knowing what to say I responded, "Ummm, ok. Seems like a pretty odd time to say that when we just ordered food and have to awkwardly sit here together until we're done eating."

"It doesn't have to be awkward," he said, "we're still friends! I like spending time with you, but I know I don't want to move to the suburbs, and I don't think this will work out in the long run."

I was fighting back tears. I wasn't upset that he was breaking up with me, it was that we were in a public place and he was using suburbia as the excuse to break up.

"Well, it's probably for the best anyway," was all I could muster.

We sat there together, him feeling relieved and trying to make small talk and making light of the awkward as hell situation we were in.

"Why didn't you just do this at your house before we committed to going to dinner?" I asked, still so confused as to why he would do this here, now.

"I don't really know, but we're still friends, so we can enjoy dinner as friends." was all he had to say about it.

Again, I found myself staying in an unhealthy relationship for far too long, putting up with things just because they were better and different things than I'd been through with Scott. Had my history not taught me anything? Here I was, having the other party make the decision to be done for us. It was an obvious decision, and one I should have done long ago but found myself grateful that he decided for us.

Flat Sandals

About a month after Ben had broken things off, he asked if I would meet him for lunch. I didn't want to, because what was the point? But I decided I would, mostly for something to do. He felt bad about how he ended things and wanted to apologize. It ended up being good closure, and we ended the meal with a hug and best wishes before heading our separate ways for good.

That night, I got a message from a match on Match.com, and this guy grabbed my interest from the first profile view. He was *hot*, as, in "holy shiz, this guy is sexy as hell" and I could not believe that *he* messaged *me*. I mean, I'd sent messages to hotties before, but never really expecting (nor getting) any responses because I felt I was reaching way out of my league.

But here was this guy, winking at me, and all I could think was that this was surely a mistake. I read his profile over and over, studying all of his words and pictures, and could not find one fault in any of them. There was the picture of him and his son, maybe 3 at the time, on the beach playing in the ocean. Such a simple photo of a moment shared with father and son, but that picture showed me a piece of his world. It was a candid photo with neither of them even noticing a camera, which meant someone took that photo of them because they noticed the beauty of the moment, too. The sheer bliss on the child's face, the dad, clearly in his element and loving being in this moment with his boy.

Another photo of this handsome man was next to who I could only presume was his father, arm around his dad, both of them with giant, beaming sunshine grins, thoroughly enjoying their time together. So, he's seemingly a family man and this was preciously evident in the pictures he chose to share about himself. He was brilliantly honest and forthcoming with who he was and what he was looking for in a partner, and all of it was me. I thought there was no way I could sell myself enough to have him respond again, so I just started with a "Hello." That was about all I could muster because I was afraid it would just fall into a black hole somewhere.

I checked my messages constantly, fully expecting to never see a reply. But there it was, a "hello" back. I was beyond giddy at this point. He's responding! We sent a few messages back and forth with mostly basic info like work, what type of food do you like, let's be Facebook friends, etc. before finally setting up a first date. Even in our brief message interaction, I was excited to know more about this man and to figure out how he could possibly want to know more about me. He was witty and funny and engaging, and so far, I was grateful for the chance to meet him.

When setting up our first date, Kevin said it would need to be a late start because he had to work late that day, so we agreed to meet for a drink at 9 pm. Here's where my past crept in. My initial reaction was to think he just *said* he had to work late, but probably had a dinner date lined up already and planned to meet me after that. I was still so insecure and cynical, but nothing that he'd said, or didn't say, should have made me question his intentions.

I was so excited to be meeting him but so very cautious at the same time. This felt too good to be true, and I had been dealt a lot of heartaches before. This was just a first date and nothing was riding on it, so what was I so worried about? I offered some options of where we could meet, but he replied that it was up to me and that I should choose.

I was a little annoyed by this because I hate making decisions, and what if I picked the wrong place? But I also thoroughly dislike ambivalence and indecisiveness, so I decided on the place and we agreed to meet there at 9 pm. Turned out, he was new to dating too. After being married for fifteen years, he was just as clueless as I was as to how you date when your world as you knew it got turned upside down.

Since our date didn't begin until 9 pm, my night began with our annual cousins' night, where all the adult women cousins get together with food and wine and sit around, chat, and play board games. I was so blasé about going on the date because I hadn't been having great luck and was starting to get annoyed with the whole dating process. There are usually around ten cousins at our gatherings, which means plenty of things to gossip about, but not surprisingly, my impending first date was the highlight of discussion. My dear cousins wanted nothing more than for me to meet a fantastic man that would care for me in all the ways I deserved but hadn't yet found. After my experiences with Scott, they knew I needed someone extra special.

When it was finally time for me to leave to meet him, I was still feeling a little reluctant. "It's so late and it's already been such a long day, how long will I last in conversation?" Looking back, it wasn't for lack of excitement about the date, it was about protecting myself from being hurt. I had been ecstatic about the chance to meet this man, so why was I suddenly feeling nonchalant about it? Truth was, I was scared and nervous and also, maybe far too hopeful.

I don't think I even got really "ready" for the date after cousin's night. I mean, I definitely primped, but I guess I just felt comfortable about this date. I normally want to get gussied up and put my best face forward, spending hours picking out the right outfit, including the sexy underwear, the right shoes, making sure my hair and makeup are perfect and that I smell beautiful. But hey, this was just drinks at a local bar, right? No need to get gussied up!

I was wearing skinny jeans and a neon-pink satin t-shirt with flat sandals. Who wears flat sandals to a first date? They were cute, shimmery gold, strappy sandals, but still *sandals*. To be honest, there was a real reason why I wore flat shoes; the last couple guys I'd gone out with claimed to be 5' 10" but had come barely above eye-level to me and my 5' 6" frame, which means they thought they were taller than they were. I didn't like wearing heels only to end up being as tall or taller than the guy I was with, so when I read that this guy was also 5' 10", I took preventative measures and wore the flat shoes.

I have been 5' 6" my entire adult life, which seems only slightly taller than average, yet most people consider me tall or don't believe that I'm *only* five and a half feet tall. I've learned that it's because I have very long legs that make me seem taller than I am. That, and the fact that I'm almost always in heels.

As I drove to the bar from cousin's night, it almost felt routine. Dating shouldn't feel routine, should it? Some people love dating and meeting new people; I discovered that I didn't like it too much. I loathe small talk and I find it extremely uncomfortable to talk about myself. I'm terrified of pauses in conversation and feel like it is my responsibility to find a new topic when a lull appears. I also severely dislike walking into a place alone, having to look around for the person I am there to meet. It's so awkward wandering around scanning the room for the person you are there to see, especially if you've only known what this person looks like via specifically chosen pictures on their dating profile.

But I'm a capable adult, and I walked into the (unusually quiet for a Saturday night) restaurant and saw him sitting along the bar, facing the entrance so he was easily noticeable. He wasn't looking in my direction, but at the TVs above the bar, likely catching up on some sports game stats. This allowed me to check him out for a minute to be sure it was actually him. I suddenly panicked that I hadn't put my best effort into my appearance for this date. He was so handsome sitting there, his dark hair and neatly trimmed beard, sun-kissed skin from the summer that was coming to an end.

He was wearing a black t-shirt, the dressy kind, that showed off his muscular arms and built physique; not in a body-builder way, but in the "I work out regularly" way. I don't know if he had seen me out of the corner of his eye, knowing I was soon approaching him, but as I was almost standing next to him, I asked, "Kevin?" and he seemed almost a little startled. After he acknowledged that he was the hottie I'd seen online (and now right in front of me!), I leaned in and gave him a giant squeeze of a hug. I don't think he expected it, and I think he was much more nervous than I was, but he returned the gesture politely.

He had already ordered a beer, which meant that he had gotten there a little early, which I found respectful. He asked me what I'd like to drink, and in true me fashion, I didn't have an answer. I've been legally drinking for over fifteen years, yet every time it comes to order it's like I forget what my options are! I said that I would just have what he was having.

We moved out to the patio as it was a beautiful, August night. Standing face to face, I realized he must be the 5'10" he said he was because I was definitely looking up at him. And what a sight he was!

The band must've been on a break when I first got there because suddenly, the music was very loud and there were a lot of people around. We decided to go back into the restaurant portion where no one else was. We sat at the empty tables which were covered in butcher paper so kids could color on them, talking about our kids and work and normal first date conversation. It was so effortless, and we found a lot to talk about. I didn't even feel like I had to fill a lull, I was just comfortable being there.

As it neared midnight, we decided to say our goodbyes before the bar got too crazy, and also because we're single parents who work full time and are typically in bed after the evening news. He walked slowly behind me as he walked me to my car, as if he didn't want the night to end, or that he was nervous about what to do next. We stood for a minute, thanking each other for a good time chatting, and then hugged goodnight. While it was comfortable, it was a little hard to read. Did he like me? Would we go on another date? Regardless, I had had a great time and was thrilled I got the chance to meet him.

Kevin and I went on a couple more dates, each one becoming more and more comfortable, like we'd known each other forever. The second date ended with a long goodbye hug, with both of us unsure of what to do next. While at the stoplight after leaving, I got a text from Kevin that said, "I wanted to kiss you soooooo badly!"

I responded, "I wanted you to, sooooo badly!"

We laughed about it and agreed we would kiss on the next date, which is an odd thing, isn't it? Planning a kiss? I guess we were too nervous to chance a good thing. For our third date, Kevin asked if I wanted to meet him at his house after work and we could order pizza and watch a movie. Nights in at home are my favorite, and I was thrilled to take him up on the offer. He lived about thirty minutes from me, and we planned to meet at his house at 7. I was done with work early and decided to order the pizza before I left my house so that I could pick it up by his house, that way we didn't have to wait even longer to have dinner. I grabbed a six-pack of beer and the pizza and rang his doorbell to signal my arrival.

"Dinner's here!" Kevin opened the door to find me with pizza and beer in hand and he could not have had a bigger smile. Taking the goods from my hands, he walked me into the kitchen where he set down our dinner, then continued back toward my direction. He took my hands in his, leaned in, and kissed me. Kevin's hazel eyes are like magic, looking through me into my soul, igniting my whole being on fire, wanting more of everything with him.

"You sure know the way to a man's heart!" he joked, enjoying that I had planned ahead.

We sat on the cool, cream leather couch, enjoying our dinner while talking through some comedy movie; we've always had hours-long conversations, fueling our intimacy.

After about six weeks and several more dates, Kevin asked me if I wanted to go with him to Las Vegas to celebrate his upcoming fortieth birthday.

"Sure, I'd love to!" was my reply, which shocked him quite a bit.

There we were, planning a long weekend away in Vegas where I'd meet his friends and family for the first time after only knowing him for three months. His siblings lived in Denver, but were meeting us in Vegas to celebrate his birthday. He had friends that lived in Vegas, along with several from home that would be joining us as well.

Normally, I think this would be intimidating for anyone, meeting a whole gaggle of people you feel the need to impress, but I liked Kevin a lot and was thrilled to be meeting the people he loved the most. Wherever we went, Kevin took my hand and made sure I was comfortable. He introduced me as "Jess," as if everyone had already heard all about me, beaming with happiness as he said it. He was happy to have me by his side, and he made me feel loved and special, even though we were there to celebrate him.

Part of me thought we might find ourselves at a little white Vegas chapel, having a quickie wedding ceremony, and I wouldn't have said no! I think we both knew that we had a good thing going. I loved everyone I met, instantly, and they were happy that Kevin and I were in love. On the car ride back home after returning from Vegas, we held hands and could hardly contain our smiles.

His hand resting warmly on my thigh, Kevin looked over at me and asked, "So what now? Should we look for a house?"

We laughed together because it seemed ridiculous that we didn't want to spend another minute apart, but it was true; we had quickly fallen madly in love. We made it about six whole months before trying to seriously commit and began looking for a house we could blend our families into. He had bought his current house only three years before, when he'd gotten divorced. It was a five-bedroom house, which he shared with his two kids half the time. Their mom lived about a mile down the road and the kids split their time between the two houses.

The house certainly had enough room for all of us, his two kids and my two boys, but it felt like we'd be moving into their space, which didn't feel like home to me. We spent a lot of time looking for houses for sale in the area, knowing we'd have to stay near his children's mom. The small town with a small school district was thirty minutes away from where I lived with the boys and given our need for a good special education program, I had a big decision to make.

I made an appointment to meet with the principal of the school that Joey would attend and invited Kevin to join me. He declined because he wanted me to feel like I could ask any questions concerning the school without being worried that he might influence my decision. I appreciated the sentiment, even though I knew he'd support whatever decision I'd make.

"I want you to make the best decision for yourself and the boys, and I'll be here no matter what." I knew he meant it. I knew that we didn't have to move just to be with him, and if I wasn't comfortable, we would live apart until the time was right.

I graduated high school with over five hundred kids in my class, and the school district in which we currently lived the class sizes were over eight hundred. I was used to larger districts with a lot of extra-curricular opportunities, but was now evaluating a district with just over a hundred kids in each class and was nervous that they wouldn't have the special education support we needed for Joey.

I met with the principal and the special ed team, toured the school, and was pleasantly surprised. I felt comfortable that they would take good care of us and was confident in the decision to join our families together, under one roof. Kevin had made it clear to me that he didn't want to get married again, and I was okay with that. He had been in a long-term relationship since high school, married for fifteen years before he caught his wife having an affair. I'd been there, done that, and marriage hadn't worked out for me either; I didn't need to be married to be fulfilled.

A few months had gone by and we still hadn't been able to find any houses that would suit our family, so we decided to look into building our own. It was spring by now, and the Parade of Homes was currently going on. We spent our weekends parading through designer-built homes, sometimes bringing the kids, sometimes touring solo, trying to find the house we could imagine our family of six feeling at home in. Not surprisingly, we found several! So many homes were meticulously decorated and *new*, but we couldn't find a builder willing to come to our town, so our choices were limited.

Finally, our realtor was able to convince a builder friend he knew through the business to come and build our home. We chose the perfect lot in a perfectly wooded neighborhood overlooking the Minnesota River with plenty of space and nature trails for the kids to roam and explore.

Nearly one year to the day we met, the boys and I moved into Kevin's house just before the school year started so they could get acclimated while we waited for our new home to be built. The transition was effortless, and in fact, being in a smaller school setting was probably best for Joey to thrive.

Little Red Dress

It was the middle of April, leading up to a weekend when the boys would be with Scott. I had been doing a fairly intense eighty-day workout program where I did one-hour workouts six days a week and completely changed my diet. I don't normally work out regularly, but about once a year I get the motivation to start a workout regimen. The weekend ahead would culminate with day eighty, the final day of the program, happening on Saturday, and I hadn't missed a workout in three months. Well, that's not true. I started the program on January 15 and came down with influenza five days later, the day before we were leaving to take the family to Disney World. My coach and I decided that I would skip the week and make it up at the end of the eighty days if I so desired. I took that week off to not only rest but to enjoy the first-ever trip to Disney with the kids.

On Monday, Kevin mentioned that we had dinner plans on Saturday night and that it would be fancy. We didn't normally make plans ahead of time, but I was excited, especially since I would be able to celebrate the end of the eighty days. When it was a weekend without the kids, Kevin still worked on Saturdays, so I would usually make appointments for pedicures or facials or other pampering activities as my way of self-care.

"Do you have any appointments scheduled for Saturday? I'm thinking of taking Saturday off and we can just have a whole-day date." He had nervousness in his voice that I couldn't place, and wondered if there was more to the day than dinner. Maybe we'd go run errands during the day or just take the day to enjoy each other's company.

"I do, but that sounds super fun! I'll just reschedule, and we can spend the day together." I was excited that he had a fun day in mind for the two of us and was happy to reschedule my massage.

Friday morning came around and we were expecting an extremely late-season snowstorm, as in blizzard conditions and several inches of snow. Kevin needed to come clean on his plans since the storm was getting in the way.

"So, ummm, about this weekend," he stammered. "We had tickets to fly to Chicago, but our flight was canceled because of the snow."

Wow! This wasn't just a surprise day date, this was a surprise weekend getaway, a first, and I was giddy that he had something up his sleeve. We had just gotten the kids out the door to school and I was going to work from home to avoid the afternoon traffic that would no doubt be horrendous. I was leaning over the counter, watching Kevin spread the peanut butter on his toast before he headed out the door to work. He's so focused and calm no matter what he's doing, no matter how stressful the situation.

"Chicago? That would have been fun. What a bummer!" I tried not to sound disappointed, and I was still actually quite excited that he had tried to plan something.

"I know," he said calmly, "I was looking forward to it." Then he pondered out loud, most likely to get my reaction, "I guess we could always drive. If we leave early enough, maybe we can get ahead of the bad stuff."

I perked up. "Ok, sure! Let's see how the day pans out and we can see how the weather looks this afternoon." If he was game to drive through the snowstorm, so was I. We loved traveling and going on adventures with each other, and this was bound to be one to remember.

My workday ended at 4 pm and the snow hadn't started yet. Kevin texted to say he was leaving work a little early and would be home soon. "Ok," I responded, "I'm just going to do my work out quickly and then get packed."

My workouts were an hour-long, and then I would need to shower, so there was nothing "quick" about it. But, as always, Kevin was cool and calm and said, "Alrighty, see you soon!"

We were on the road by six, with a light dusting of snow just beginning to cover the roads.

"This isn't so bad," I said out loud, even though it was an obvious observance. I pulled up the radar and saw that we certainly weren't going to be so lucky for the rest of the trip. An hour into the drive we could hardly see in the dark, blizzard-like conditions.

"Maybe we should have waited until morning," we both acknowledged, with half a laugh, as in, we *definitely shouldn't have made the trek tonight!*

Most of the drive was highway, two lanes going in either direction, yet we couldn't even see which lane we were supposed to be in. The only vehicles on the road were large SUVs and semi-trucks, while we were in a Chevy Impala with sport tires; not an ideal choice for driving through the constant snowdrifts collecting along the way.

Kevin is an excellent navigator through the snow, confident and comfortable behind the wheel, whereas I'm terrified that the tires will slip or catch in a drift and send me off the road into the shoulder where I will not be easily retrieved. I remained silent, gripping my legs with my fingers just to put my anxiety some-where. Semis terrify me too, in daylight on a dry summer day, so to be sharing the road with them in these horrendous conditions had me in a near panic. But I had to remain calm, I was only the passenger, and there was nothing I could do about it anyway, so best to just sit quietly and let Kevin do the driving.

He noticed I wasn't handling the drive so well, of course, and tried to lighten the mood with some upbeat music or by giving my leg or hand a quick squeeze, but I just wanted to get there and be out of the car. He found his way behind a semi-truck and was able to follow in the tracks made by its tires, finally finding some contact with the road rather than inches of snow. The truck also provided light to follow rather than the pitch-black snow globe we had been trying to navigate. However, the newly found comfort we had found was soon to be gone as we saw the truck turn on its blinker to take the upcoming exit.

"Well, I think we'd be better off following him off the highway and finding a place to stay the night here." Kevin conceded. We were in a small Wisconsin town that he knew of, and it had taken us over four hours to get there; it would have only taken two in normal conditions. It was after ten o'clock and at that rate, if we had kept driving, we likely wouldn't make it to Chicago until the early morning. We were tired and it just wasn't safe to continue. We found a hotel that had vacancies, checked in, and headed to the bar across the street.

"We'll each have a shot and a beer," Kevin said to the bartender as we pulled up a stool at the bar. We laughed and told her about how awful the drive had been while she poured me a shot of vodka, chilled, and a shot of Jack Daniels for him.

"Cheers!" we said as we clinked our shot glasses before tipping back the mouthful of bitter, nerve-calming liquid.

The bartender replaced the shot glasses with bottles of Spotted Cow beer, an exclusive to Wisconsin, saying "There must be something pretty special in Chicago if you were willing to brave the storm!"

Given that I had no idea why we *were* on our way to Chicago, I just smiled and looked to Kevin for information. Then she continued, "Do you plan to propose or something?" winking at Kevin.

"Maybe!" was his reply, while I laughed and simultaneously said "Oh, no, definitely not," my gaze turned downward away from the awkwardness. Kevin had told me that he didn't want to get married again, that he felt he had failed in his first marriage and didn't want to go through that again. I was extremely comfortable with this fact and had come to understand that we would never get married; I knew I had his commitment and that he loved me more than I had ever imagined I could be loved.

We finished our beers and headed back to the hotel to get some sleep before continuing the drive in the morning. The storm hadn't let up by morning, but at least the snowplows had been out, and it was easier to see the road. After driving another four hours, we finally came into downtown Chicago. It was foggy with low clouds hiding the tops of the skyscrapers.

Passing the John Hancock building Kevin said, pointing upward, "We are heading to the top of that building for a drink at seven o'clock tonight."

Ahhhh, a start! Something concrete in our plans. I thought that we must be meeting someone there, maybe some friends or siblings were coming to join us for the night. I don't know why I thought people would be joining us, other than it seemed like we had to be there at a specific time for *something*. Seven o'clock is usually dinner time, but he said we were going there for a drink. Hmmmm, so we're not having dinner there...

By now we were close to the hotel and passed Ditka's Restaurant, owned by the famous NFL coach, Mike Ditka.

"That's where we're having dinner," Kevin said excitedly.

I responded, "Oh, how *fun!*" matching the same sarcastic tone Kevin had. We had not driven over two days to have dinner at an upscale sports bar, I knew that for sure.

Finally, we arrived at our hotel, the Sofitel Chicago, using valet to park the car. It had stopped snowing, so we were able to walk into the hotel without sloshing through the snow on the side-walks. Kevin checked us in while I waited across the lobby just in case there were things I shouldn't be hearing on this complete surprise of a trip. This was an uber fancy hotel; we had just driven hours and hours through a blizzard, and I still had no idea why we were here. Once he got the key cards to our room, we took the elevator to the twentieth floor and found our room down the hall. We opened the door, hauled our bags into the room, and while standing in the middle of the room, I pulled his face towards mine and kissed him. No matter why we had come, I was already happy to have been on this crazy trip with him this far.

It was already late afternoon, and we were both hungry. "I'll head down the street to grab us some appetizers from Ditka's if you want to take your time getting ready," Kevin suggested.

"Man, so you're saying we're not going to Ditka's for dinner?" I joked. He laughed and kissed me goodbye, heading out to go walk for food.

The only plans I knew of were that we were heading for a drink at the John Hancock building at 7 pm, which meant I had about three hours to get ready. Ready for what, exactly? Kevin had hinted that he'd like to see me in a red dress, and I had gotten one for our "fancy" Saturday night dinner he had mentioned. It was a sexy, little-red-dress type with a neckline that was lower on the left, showing some side boob, and gradually went higher into a thick strap across my right shoulder. It had a gold zipper running down the length of the left side, and while the dress was a sheath and fitted to my knees, the zipper ended right at mid-thigh, showing some leg.

Knowing he'd be back with food soon, I decided just to shower and get into the plush white robe that came with the hotel room while I waited for him. I sat on the bed looking around the room and out at the city through the floor-to-ceiling windows. I was excited for whatever was to come, but also a little unsure; what could we possibly be here for? There was a knock at the door, causing me to hop up to see who it was. Peeking out the peephole in the door I saw Kevin standing there with the "I forgot my key!" look, so I quickly opened the door and let him in.

Setting the food on the table in the hotel room, he pulled out a t-shirt he got for himself from Ditka's. He's funny like that; he loves t-shirts that say things. He got himself a memento so we could remember the time we came to Chicago to *not* have Ditka's for dinner. We took our time filling up on appetizers, realizing that more time had passed than we expected and would need to call for an Uber soon.

While Kevin was in the shower I slipped into my red dress, excited for him to see what I had packed to wear. I felt flashy, like something I would feel more comfortable wearing in Vegas, but knew I was overthinking it. I was standing at the mirror outside of the bathroom, finishing my makeup when Kevin came out of the shower. A giant grin spread across his face as he proclaimed, "Wow, babe, you look incredible!"

He slowly walked over to me, eyeing me up and down, and when he was finally close enough, he gently took my face in his hands, looked directly into my eyes to make sure I was paying attention, and said, "I love you."

And there it was; I felt absolutely beautiful and wholly loved for who I was, worthy of the love, and not just because I was wearing a sexy red dress.

We arrived promptly at the John Hancock building at 7 o'clock, as discussed. We followed the signs for the bar that would take us to the ninety-sixth floor of the building, 1,000 feet above Michigan Avenue. The elevator ride was intense, moving up the floors quickly, our ears popping along the way. Once the doors opened on the ninety-sixth floor, I expected to see people we knew standing there, waiting for us, but there wasn't a familiar face in sight. We checked in at the host stand and they brought us to a table alongside the windows so we could look out over the city. However, it was still foggy with low clouds, so we didn't have much of a view at all. Regardless, the experience was incredible.

There we were, at the one place I knew we were going for the evening, and still, nothing seemed to be happening. I ordered a lemon drop martini and Kevin, their special, an old-fashioned. We sat and chatted about the city, our drinks, and how awful his old-fashioned was, especially for them to call it their "special." Finally, I asked what we were doing here.

"So, we drove all the way here in a blizzard, do we have any other plans?" I asked, amusedly perplexed.

Kevin replied, in his best "I have a secret" tone, "We're going to dinner after this, but our reservation isn't until 8:30 pm, so I thought it would be fun to come here for a drink first."

Ahhhh, so we *are* going to be eating dinner, that's good. Otherwise, I wouldn't even think about ordering another martini, as I was already feeling the first.

"Where are we having dinner?" I asked, expecting that he might finally tell me at this point.

"It's a surprise," he said, his eyes sparkling in the dimly lit bar. The way he looked at me, with such passion and lust, distracted me and I turned away to gaze outside, unable to stop my smile.

We finished our second round of drinks by the time I needed to head back down the ninety-five floors to catch our Uber to the restaurant. All I had was the address on the map of the Uber driver's phone, which didn't give me any clues. About fifteen minutes into the drive, the driver asked, "Is this it?"

Kevin replied, unsure himself, "I think so!"

There appeared to be a neighborhood on the left side of the road and small office buildings on the right. It was dark and everything was damp from the previous days' snow. None of the buildings had signs for me to decipher where we were, so I just trusted that Kevin knew we were in the right spot. He walked ahead, holding my hand in his, leading me to the door of what I assumed was the restaurant. We walked in and were immediately greeted by two hostesses that offered to take our coats and show us to our seats. The entryway was only a hallway, with a simple, yet elegant, gray counter and small coat closet behind it.

"Right this way," the hostess walked us through the empty hall and around the corner through a floor-to-ceiling white curtain, shielding what was on the other side. I glanced at Kevin with excited eyes that shouted, "Where are we?" He just grabbed my hand and smiled.

Once we were behind the curtain, we entered a room with one large table set for sixteen people. The hostess led us around the back of the table, opposite from where we started, seating us across from another couple. I looked around the table and realized it was over half full, yet I didn't know any of them. I was confused, wondering why we'd come to a restaurant that seemed expensive, yet we had to share a table with people we didn't know.

I leaned closer to Kevin and asked, "What is this place?"

He brought my hand to his lap and said, "You know where we are!", and I assured him that I truly had no idea.

"Alinea," he said, "you know, from the Netflix show *Chef's Table?*"

My jaw dropped instantly, my eyebrows jumped for the ceiling and I had to hold my cheeks so they didn't rip open from the smile that was bursting across my face. *This! This is why we're here; why we couldn't miss this trip to Chicago!*

Chef's Table is a Netflix series that goes in-depth into the personal passion behind some of the most world-renowned chefs of our time from all over the world. Alinea was the star of one of these episodes, winning Michelin's highest accolade of three stars.

Kevin was so excited that we were finally here, and that he could finally share the surprise. I could not believe he made this happen for me! We had watched the show here and there and I had said that it was a goal of mine to get to go to one of those incredible restaurants someday, never actually thinking I *would*.

The experience was like nothing I'd ever had before; a twenty-course dinner with wine pairings specifically curated to go with each presentation. Every plate that came out had a story and an experience to be seen, smelled, and tasted. Once all sixteen people had arrived, eight waiters came out, one for every two people, delivering each of us a small tray with a foggy glass dome atop it. Steam, or fog, or smoke swirled around inside the dome making it difficult to see what was inside. After every place had been set, the waiters removed the glass, revealing a shallow bowl of creamy soup.

After the first course, the group was brought into the kitchen to watch at least ten chefs work to prepare the rest of the evening's courses. We enjoyed what they called a "gourmet hot pocket," which was a beautifully handcrafted, bite-sized flaky croissant stuffed with cheese and some Italian cured meat, topped with a delicate violet. When we returned to our table, we found it broken down into smaller, individual tables where we would enjoy the rest of the dinner as a two-some, rather than a large group. It felt like we had stepped into an entirely different room than we had previously been in.

The remaining courses were as unique as they were delicious. There were centerpieces meant to enhance the teeny tiny bites for a particular course, such as a bowl filled with sliced oranges and dry ice creating a citrus fog over the table, followed by a smoking juniper branch to enhance the next. There was a campfire center-piece that ended up being part of the next course; once the flames were extinguished the waiter dug into the "sand" (which happened to be salt) to pull out the potatoes that had been cooking in the heated salt since early that morning. The courses just kept coming, each one continuing to amaze.

Towards the end of the three-hour meal, the waiters used step ladders to remove the décor that had been hanging above us on the ceiling. They placed the table-sized "plates" (décor) in front of us while other waiters walked around spooning creams, chocolates, and puddings onto the plates for us to dip our desserts in.

As we were finishing up our second dessert, which was an edible balloon filled with helium, served with an immaculate chocolate mousse that had been coated and shaped to look exactly like a small banana, the waiter dropped off the next centerpiece on our table. It appeared to be a large, evergreen branch set on top of a birch tree stump, and I noticed that it seemed to be growing, raising itself from the stump. I looked around and realized that none of the other tables had this newly delivered centerpiece, but I was also three hours into a twenty-course meal with several paired beverages alongside, so I wasn't too aware of what was going on around us.

Kevin and I continued to talk about how absolutely fantastic the experience had been, reminiscing on the drive that got us there. After a few minutes, I noticed that the branch on the table had, in fact, risen, and there appeared to be a chocolate box on the stump previously covered by the leaves on the branch.

"Oh, look, there's something else. What is it?" I asked as Kevin went to grab it, unsure himself.

"Actually, why don't you get it?" he asked, urging me to take the box instead.

I took the box off the stump, excited to try the next course in our meal. The box was black and about three inches square, looking just like it would contain small bites of some decadent chocolates. I pulled off the top of the box and for the second time that night, my jaw fell to my lap and I looked up to see Kevin kneeling next to the table, reaching for my hand. There was a *beautiful* diamond solitaire ring staring at me from the box.

"I lied," he said emotionally, "I *do* want to get married again. Will you marry me, please?"

Absolutely unable to contain my excitement, and complete

surprise, I pulled him off the floor and next to me in our booth, kissing his face over and over.

"Wait, did you say yes?" he asked, realizing I hadn't verbalized a response.

"Yes! Absolutely, yes!" I exclaimed, my cheeks feeling tight from all of the smiling I'd done for the past few hours.

When we woke up the next morning, Kevin felt for my left hand in the bed, finding that the engagement ring was still on my finger.

"So, it wasn't a dream." He stated rather than questioned. And we held each other, knowing we were the most perfect pair there ever was.

Kevin told me later that he had called my dad while on his walk to Ditka's for appetizers to ask his permission to marry me. I think it was more out of tradition, and a sign of respect, but also, Kevin is a family-man and wanted to bring our families closer together.

We got engaged on April 15 and were set to close and move into our brand-new house within a month. I hadn't planned that we would also be getting married in that timeframe as well, but we didn't want to wait to be married to each other; we wanted to move into our new home as a married couple, as a family. Neither of us cared about a typical, formal wedding and decided we would just get hitched at the courthouse. Except then realized we needed adult witnesses to our ceremony and ran into the problem of trying not to hurt anyone's feelings. We couldn't have just one of our moms there without the other, and we couldn't have friends but no family, so we decided on a small Sunday ceremony at a local park gazebo with a justice of the peace instead.

The date of our wedding was set for Sunday, May 6, at three o'clock in the afternoon. Our invitation consisted of a text or a phone call simply asking our closest friends and family to join us. The guest list was fewer than thirty people, and they all confirmed they "wouldn't miss it!" The reception would be simple, taking place at the bar/restaurant where we had our first date, serving a casual taco and pizza bar.

All I had to do now was to find a wedding dress, which just needed to be any dress that would look appropriate for an outdoor park wedding. I asked my friend Courtney to come shopping with me, along with my fifteen-year-old soon-to-be step-daughter, Anabelle, and we ventured to the Mall of America, as it would have the most extensive options for a dress.

I envisioned some sort of white-ish color, maybe with some beading or lace or something that said, "wedding dress," but I wanted it to be tea-length or shorter because it was just a casual affair, after all. I was struggling; I couldn't find anything in the white-ish family that spoke to me. Eventually, we stumbled into Armani Exchange, which is not a place I would normally find myself, however, I remembered a time Scott brought me there because he thought it was a cool, expensive brand. I had found a few things then, on the seventy percent off rack, so I figured it was worth a stop in.

We made our way through the store, ending up at the back in the clearance section where I spotted a dress highlighted on the wall. It was navy, almost opposite of white, but I kept being drawn to it. I walked over and pulled it off the rack, draping it over my front to see how it would fall. The girls came closer and started "Ooohing" and urging me to try it on, just to see. We scanned the rack for my size but had no such luck; they had a size smaller or two sizes too large, but I decided to go for it and try the size too small.

I shrugged and said to the collective group, "You never know, different brand's sizes mean different things," trying to convince myself that maybe those eighty days of workouts had paid off.

I went into the fitting room to put the dress on, feeling

nervous because the only dress I had found so far wasn't even in my size. But I was also excited, I was here to find a dress to marry the most perfect man with whom to spend the rest of my life, and I hardly cared about the dress I would wear to do so. I put the dress on and stared at myself in the mirror for a minute.

"Sooooo, it fits," I said to Courtney and Anabelle over the curtain closing off my changing room, "but I'm not sure if it's a *wedding* dress."

I pulled back the curtain and stepped out so they could see me.

"I love it!" Courtney squealed, clapping her hands and grinning wildly.

"Yea, it's really pretty," agreed Anabelle.

The dress was dark navy blue in a stretchy scuba-type fabric, very fitted at the top with wider tank-style straps, and it flowed out at the waist into a pleated bell-like shape, ending at mid-thigh. The bottom of the dress was scalloped with little flower cutouts that ran along the edges; classic, a little bit 1950s housewife with a modern, sexy twist, and I kinda loved it. It was shorter than I expected to be wearing, and certainly tighter in the bust due to it being a size too small, but the three of us agreed that it was "the one." So, I bought my wedding dress off the clearance rack at Armani Exchange for sixty-five bucks. And it was a good thing because the wedding was only a week away.

The Fastest "I Do"

The love I'd found in Kevin wasn't the lustful, fleeting type of love; it's the fulfilling, endless love that completes your soul. When you first become a parent with a new baby, you discover a love you never knew existed, that you could be so blessed to know. That's how it was with us: pure, true, and whole. Our love story deserves to be told.

The morning of our wedding day, I got up early to visit the local flower shop in town to pick out some white flowers for the centerpiece at our greeting table. I didn't want a bridal bouquet, and there weren't any bridesmaids, but flowers make anything prettier. I picked out a few white roses and tulips and added in some greenery, asking the clerk to wrap a white silk ribbon around the stems.

"What's the occasion?" the florist asked.

"Well, I'm getting married today and wanted something pretty for the ceremony," I replied simply, amused by her surprise in the simplicity of it.

Kevin and our three boys went to pick up the folding chairs we had rented locally and set them up over at the park's gazebo. Anabelle and I stayed home so that my soon-to-be mother-in-law could style our hair. As she was curling my hair to pin it up in loose curls, I thought about how all of this was really for everyone else; that they would be the ones to be upset if we had just gone to the courthouse. But Kevin and I knew this, and we knew that as long as we got to be husband and wife, it didn't matter how we got there.

Once our hair was finished and we put on our dresses, the three of us drove over to meet the boys at the park, only a few minutes before everyone else was scheduled to arrive. I set up a table at the entrance into the gazebo, placing a large rustic metal beverage tub in the center full of ice and bottles of sparkling wine. I had found champagne flutes dressed as a bride and groom for Kevin and me to use to celebrate the occasion, while everyone else would use plastic disposable champagne flutes. The only other thing on the table was the flowers I had picked up that morning; simple, romantic, and fun.

Our family and friends had started to trickle in, all of us mingling ahead of the ceremony. The justice of the peace, Kelly, got there right on time, which was about twenty minutes after the guests were asked to arrive. Kelly stood at the front of the rows of arranged chairs, signaling for everyone to take their seats. Our four kids sat together in the front row on one side, while everyone else sat wherever they pleased; there were no rules to this ceremony, just effortless simplicity. Kevin and I made our way to the back of the group, standing at the start of the aisle, ready to finalize our commitment to each other.

Without waiting a minute too long, we cheerfully made our way down the aisle together, waving and smiling at our guests as we went. There wasn't any pomp and circumstance, no music to march to the beat to, just the peaceful sound of trees swaying in the breeze, birds chattering, and children playing off in the distance. There were only about four rows of guests, so it didn't take us too long to make it to the front where Kelly was already standing.

Neither of us had written any vows because we'd already said everything we felt about each other in private. People could see how we loved each other just by watching us, we didn't need to express it verbally to *them*. It was also out of respect to our children, not wanting to inadvertently embarrass them or make them doubt our previous lives with their other parents. Kelly hadn't prepared any sort of speech either but recited a poem about the magnitude of love worth choosing. Kevin and I held hands, watching Kelly speak, waiting for the moment she asked us to say our "I dos."

"Do you, Kevin, take Jessica to be your wife, in sickness and in health?" She asked him.

"I do, of course." was his reply.

"Do you, Jessica, take Kevin to be your husband, in sickness and in health?" It was my turn.

"Yes, I do, absolutely!" I exclaimed.

"Well, by the State of Minnesota I pronounce you husband and wife!" was her last line delivered to us.

I reached up to Kevin's face and pulled him to mine, kissing him through my smile that I couldn't contain. His hands were around my waist, pulling me toward him, and we were embraced in love and happiness. After a few kisses, we turned towards our guests and I announced, "Well, that's it!" and laughed along with them.

"That was the shortest and most awesome wedding I've *ever* been to!" was the sentiment repeated throughout the rest of the afternoon. And it was truly everything we could have asked for, even though we had originally preferred not to have any of it. But it was ours, and it was perfectly special.

Co-Parenting With a Narcissist

E ven though I was now married to the love of my life, raising our four kids together, and enjoying the life we were building, I was still tied to Scott because of our boys. Scott had hoped that I would move away to California when I was traveling a lot for work, saying it would be a "dream come true." That would have solved his obligation to see his children regularly and mean less time "dealing" with me. I knew that if I hadn't pushed him to see our boys, they would not have a relationship; he would have just disappeared.

The tables had turned since the divorce; I was now the one in control, even if it took me years to realize it. He hated me for it. I held him accountable by making him follow the rules, the legal ones, the rules that he couldn't pay someone off to make go away. He'd tried, hiring expensive lawyers, but thankfully we lived in a state with a decent court system. Also, Scott moved on quickly in his relationships, having less and less time to terrorize me.

When Scott was first with Kat, I didn't know what to expect. I didn't know Scott to be a caretaker and I was worried about what the time he had with the boys would look like. I was grateful that

Kat was there too, but I didn't know what she would be like as a fill-in for me. Scott requested that I meet Kat for coffee so that I could get to know her, "since she'll be helping to raise our boys." I didn't want any part of it. He had been with her during our marriage, and I could not find it in me to be friends with her.

Once Kat and Scott were engaged, he told me that it was "cute" that she and I would share his last name. I had kept the name for the sake of the boys, to be connected with them, but he tormented me about it. He hated that I didn't go back to my maiden name. Whenever he'd have to write me a check or send me something in the mail, he always used my maiden name instead of his out of spite. I was grateful to now be associated with Kevin by name, rather than him.

Co-parenting with someone that can't see beyond their own needs was sometimes impossible. I considered myself incredibly fortunate that I got sole physical custody, and that Scott chose to see them on an every-other-weekend only basis, rarely seeing them more than forty-eight hours at a time. He wasn't capable of it. He could not tolerate being alone with his kids, always needing someone else around to help him do the parenting.

The forty-eight-hour rule for him was pretty hard and fast. There were times here and there where he'd taken them for an extra day or two, but not without it being an ordeal. After he brought the boys home one day early, I sent him a text, "You have a 48-hour rule and that's it. Pretty predictable and comical, but like always, it's fine."

His response, "Why not be happy I'm in their lives? Why not be happy they love seeing me? Why not be happy they have my parents that love seeing them? Why not be happy that I pay you every month?"

I can be happy about all of those things while also loathing you for not wanting to spend time with your children.

Father's Day came a week after he'd had them for a four-day

weekend. I hadn't heard from Scott as to whether he had plans to see them for what should've been his holiday, so I sent him a text. "Will you want the boys on Sunday?"

He replied, "Just had them for four days. I love them to death, but it's too much driving for only one day."

I said I love them, so that makes up for not spending Father's Day with them.

Just as in his everyday life, Scott had grand plans for what his boys should do in life. He had no real idea what their interests or capabilities were but wanted them to do over-the-top things, like taking DJ courses to learn how to become a famous YouTuber. We lived in a small town of nearly seven thousand people, forty-five minutes away from a major city. The boys were in sports, enjoying basketball, baseball, and football. They had tutoring, guitar lessons, and summer camps. But these activities weren't special enough. He'd tried to sign Joey for specialized day camps for kids with ADHD, which if he were to attend, he would've been away from home from 7 am to 6 pm, five days a week the entire summer.

"I had an assistant do some research on summer programs for Joey." Scott texted me.

"A car picks him up every day at 7 am, he's given a snack in the car and then provided all meals for the day. The driver brings him home promptly at 6 pm."

I'm not sure if he realized that we liked having Joey home, that he was thriving, getting all As, and starting to make friends at school. Not to mention, we didn't live in some metropolis like New York, where things like that might be considered normal. But it was great you had an "assistant" do some "research" for your child.

Scott hadn't been involved in any of the medical or school evaluations for Joey in all of the years we'd been doing them. He avoided it completely, not wanting to know that his son was different. And not accepting it, nor learning anything about his diagnoses, meant he didn't have a clue about the progress his child had made.

After receiving the evaluation results in the mail, Scott texted me, saying "Did you read the packet yesterday? By no means is his social skills great." Nor are your English skills pal, but you consider yourself successful.

I replied, extremely irritated at his ignorance of his son's abilities, "You do understand that the boys are my life, my top priority, right? All the improvement we've seen with Joey didn't happen because I 'didn't read the packet...' of course I read it. I've been to every single meeting for the past six years."

His intellectual response followed, "This is what you wanted and asked for. You do realize this is what divorce means, right? You wanted top dollar child support which means I have the kids twelve percent of the time."

Again, parenting is only something he had to do because money was involved. He saw no value in it otherwise.

Child support had been a never-ending battle since we divorced. He was almost always behind, even though I enlisted the help of the county to collect payments from the very beginning and he had an incredibly well-paying job. Every single year he had fallen behind at some point, and I was so grateful to have a great job where I didn't have to rely on his support monthly. We've gone to court at least five times in the last six years; he's always fighting to reduce his support obligation, yet has never tried to counter it by requesting more visitation with his kids.

Recently, he was behind in support by about six months when I'd finally had enough. Scott would pick up the boys for his weekends in his flashy Maserati car, traveled frequently to his vacation home in Florida, and bought his newest fiancé a three-carat engagement ring, yet he didn't have any money for the county to take for child support because he had to be hiding it; I think he created different businesses to funnel income to that made it hard for the county to track.

I contacted an attorney based on a recommendation from a good friend that had recently gone through a divorce. She was expensive, but I didn't care, I wanted to prove a point. I was stuck with large attorney's fees all because he chose not to do what he was legally required to do. We filed a motion that he was in contempt of court for actively not paying support when he had every ability to do so. As soon as we asked for a discovery on all sources of income, he suddenly became current in child support, paying nearly fifteen thousand dollars in back support at once.

I was sick of fighting him constantly, but if I didn't hold him accountable, I wasn't being fair to our boys. I always said that the child support I got from him went to our kids in hopes to help make up for the time they missed with their dad. It's been used for family vacations or special gifts, but most of it went into savings to help with the bigger expenses as they get older.

Scott always said, "You better be saving the money I'm paying you because I'm not paying a dime for their cars or college."

Child support isn't supposed to be for those things, and he just didn't understand that kids need things like clothes, school supplies, daycare, food, health insurance, etc. Everything I'd done since they'd been born was to try to give them a happy and healthy home, despite the battle I faced from the other side. It was impossible to communicate with Scott, and I limited my interaction with him to simple and short text messages. Phone conversations opened up the possibility of negotiation, and coercive controlling behavior, so I refused to talk to him outside of written communication. My attorney agreed that I should not talk to him outside of a text or email, and she also would not answer his endless, abusive phone calls, rather requesting the information be presented by email.

I texted Scott to let him know that David was invited to a birthday party that would fall on a Saturday with him. "David got invited to a birthday party at the bowling alley next Saturday at 11:30. Maybe you and Joey could bowl while he's there? Joey has two basketball games after the party."

He responded, bringing up our court situation at the time. "Ok. Isn't it funny how I always just do whatever you say and never push back, but you won't simply respond to my updated child support offer to you?"

My reply was, "We will always have to communicate when it comes to the boys and their activities. As I've said, I will not discuss nor negotiate any 'deal' with you outside of my attorney."

Well, that pissed him off. He responded again, "Yes, I know, you've said it forty times. Stop texting me about the kids. Stop asking me how I can help you. Stop asking my parents for help. I have already told them to never respond to you without my approval."

Typical narcissist behavior - demanding and controlling. I didn't ask him for help. I didn't ask his parents for help. I offered them time to see the boys when they asked, but Scott saw any time with the boys as helping me, and he didn't think I deserved the "help." I was glad his parents were smart enough to not listen to him and his demands to not communicate with me. I was happy they had grandparents that loved them so much, and they were a great asset in the boys' lives.

Scott still lied about anything and everything, and occasionally I still fell for it, but I became wiser. It was easy for me to get caught up in his lies because I believed people said the truth. Because of his constant lies, I found myself becoming cynical, questioning people's motives. One sunny day this past summer when the boys were with him, I sent him a text around 11 am asking if we could meet an hour later than normal for pickup (5 pm) as we had something going on for Anabelle.

He responded, "Sure. We're going out on the boat all day anyway, so that works."

Scott owned a boat that he usually kept at his parent's lake place and took the boys there a couple of times a summer. When I picked up the boys that evening, I asked them how their day on the boat was. They both looked at me with confusion.

"We didn't go on the boat." Joey and David both responded in unison.

"Really?" I asked, letting them know that dad had said they'd be out on the boat all day.

David replied, "Dad sold the boat." to which Joey agreed.

Why did Scott tell me they'd be on the boat all day if he didn't even have the boat anymore? Did he feel like he had to compete for a *cooler* reason to be late for pickup? These were the lies that made it hard to see what was real. It was a sunny day, they'd been on the boat a few times before, there was no need to question whether that was a plausible event.

Scott and Kat had been married for about a year, but the boys said they fought often; Kat was frequently not home when it was their weekend with Joey and David, instead with friends or her sister. I liked to imagine that she left Scott alone with the boys to help foster their relationship as father and sons, and I knew it was good for her to maintain relationships outside of hers with Scott, but it also seemed odd for newlyweds to spend so much time apart. Eventually, Scott tired of Kat, and we were introduced to a new name during time with dad, Hannah.

There was no nickname to go along with Hannah, so it was just assumed we were to call her Hannah. I knew Scott was having an affair with Hannah because he'd bring her around the boys in places Kat was not. Scott asked to take our boys to a water park for a weekend getaway, to which I discovered it was Hannah there and not Kat.

It became more and more frequent that the boys were seeing Hannah instead of Kat, and I started to have to ask which woman's house I would be picking the boys up from. I knew what was happening and I disliked every minute of it, but there was nothing I could do about it; he was their dad. I hated that he couldn't provide consistency and that he was showing them a life where it was ok to jump from one relationship to the next, flip-flopping back and forth, oftentimes within a two-week period. But I also knew that they had me to provide consistency and guidance most of the time.

Others close to him saw the patterns, but it didn't make sense to them. I got asked frequently if these women were "dumb" or "stupid" to fall for him. "She must be an idiot to stay with him/get involved with a married man." They see beautiful, intelligent women that lose themselves for him, all of them leaving the life they had for him.

My answer was always the same, "They only know what he tells them."

These women were wonderful women apart from him. In other circumstances, we might have been friends, but I couldn't let myself connect with them; he didn't keep them around long, and they were, by circumstances, an extension of him. I had no idea what he told them about me, and I only knew them from the image he painted. It seemed like Kat was scared of me, and I knew he likely taught her to be intimidated by me as a way to have control over her. Did he compare her parenting abilities to mine? I didn't know the details of what brought the demise of their relationship and the introduction of Hannah; I didn't care, and it wasn't my place.

When I was single, I thought that the boys were maybe missing out on having a father figure in their lives, and I pushed to make sure their dad spent time with them. I also thought that maybe spending time with his kids would make him *want* to spend time with them too. But I was happy things worked out the way they did and that his influence on them was mostly minimal. They enjoyed getting to see him when they did, but they never complained about not seeing him enough.

Once Kevin entered our lives, they had an incredible male role model; one that asked table manners of them, helped them with homework and school projects, asked them to respect their mother, and most importantly, showed them true, unconditional, fatherly love.

The Midnight Kiss

I don't know how I was able to move on with my life, unscathed by my less-than-healthy relationship with men, but somehow, I was able to meet the man that has filled in every part of my fractured soul with love and happiness. I only hope we can teach our kids how to be loved like this. It seems like such a simple task; show them love and they will know love. However, they also need to know how to recognize the bad love. Kevin and I have both been through a divorce, only to come out on the other side realizing we had no idea what we thought love was. What we've found in each other is unexplainable, other than to say it's simply perfect. But what is perfect for us isn't what's perfect for others. My hope for our kids is that they know how to recognize what they need out of a relationship.

My parents went through a divorce when I was in my early twenties, shortly after I had met Scott. It was really hard for me to separate them from me. Their divorce was completely unexpected and surprised everyone, and I didn't know how I could be in a relationship when what I'd thought I'd known about love and marriage wasn't true. I didn't know anyone that had been through a divorce, and I knew it was frowned upon.

I ended up staying in my relationship with Scott because I thought he loved me. He took care of me, had a good job, a nice car, and his own place to live. He was fun and funny and let me not think about what was going on with my parents. However, my parents were so absorbed in their own life crises that they weren't able to help me recognize the signs of my doomed relationship. Not that I would've listened to them anyway; what did they possibly know about love?

When Kevin and I first started dating, we were separately asked the same question by those that love us, including ourselves, "Are you worried about trust?"

We'd both been in long-term marriages that ended with our spouses having affairs. The assumption is that we'd carry trust issues into relationships that came after, but for some reason, we both knew better. We knew that our ex-spouses' infidelities were due to their own issues and insecurities and that most people are good. Except that's not even really true either, good people can still get caught up in a situation and make bad decisions. People make mistakes, and sometimes couples can work through those mistakes, including building trust again after an affair.

Maybe we both finally found *the one* and it just worked out for us. Maybe we learned signs to look for in a dishonest person or a bad relationship. Whatever the reason, Kevin and I have implicit trust, and our relationship is one to stay. We stand in the kitchen, arms around each other just enjoying the embrace, listening to the competing tick and tock of the clocks around us, appreciating what life has brought us.

The sweetest thing about my husband is that when he tells a story about someone, he often describes them as "the most talented/brilliant/nicest person you'll ever meet!"

He sees the good first, always. But the truth is, *he* is one of those people too. He's kind, friendly, intelligent and intellectual, and everyone he meets considers him a friend, instantly. Kevin appreciates life and wants to make sure people know that he appreciates them in his life too. He says things like, "I don't mind cleaning up after dinner, because it means I had a nice meal to eat." and "Yes, go take a trip just to write, I'll hold down the fort at home." He supports me no matter what, even if that means he has to take the kids to doctor's visits, make dinner every night, and cart the kids where they need to be.

A good friend, Kelly, and I recently reconnected and I found out that she had just gone through a divorce herself. I felt so sad that I couldn't be there for her as she was for me when I was going through mine, but I also understood how lonely and isolating divorce is.

She started to tell me her story while we were out for a glass of wine one late afternoon but had to stop as sorrowful tears welled in her eyes. No matter how a divorce comes about, there are countless ways to feel about it: loss of what was and what could or should be, sadness and grief, or maybe happiness. All of these feelings mixed together are not easy to process all at once and can come flooding out in ways and times you least expect. I told her that it was ok and that we didn't have to talk about it here and now, or ever, if she wasn't up for it. As friends often do, we picked up as we had left off and she welcomed my new family into her home with open arms.

Kelly invited us to her house for New Year's Eve, spending the last day of 2019 together. The kids and I showed up in time to have an appetizer-style dinner, where the boys were free to roam the house with the ten other kids there, while the adults chatted around the kitchen. Kevin met me there after work, which meant we both had to drive home and there wouldn't be much celebrating by champagne toasts. We ended up leaving shortly before midnight because the little kids were tired and worn out from their sugar high.

Kelly's house sat at the end of a very narrow and windy gravel driveway. It had recently snowed several inches, which left the driveway covered in a slick coating of compacted snow with plowed mounds of snow alongside it. I was following Kevin down the driveway as we left the party and found myself unable to correct after sliding into a slippery turn. My car got just stuck enough into one of those mounds of snow that I couldn't back out of it. Kevin was already out to the main road when I called him to come back and try to help me out. But he turned around quickly and came to try to push me out. No such luck. The car wouldn't budge.

Thankfully, there were some teenage boys still back at the party and they were more than happy to bring down their shovels and buckets of sand. The three of them, plus Kevin, were able to get me back on the right path. We said our thank-yous and good-byes (again!) and headed home. Minutes down the road, Kevin stopped at a four-way stop, got out of the car, and jogged to my driver's side window, where I was stopped behind his car. I rolled down the window to ask what's up when he leaned in, kissed me, and said, "Happy New Year!" I looked at the clock and sure enough, it was midnight.

He just as quickly ran back to his car and started on his way home. Tears instantly ran down my cheeks as I thanked the universe for bringing this man, with a beautiful soul and heart of gold into my life. Not ten minutes earlier he was knee-deep in the snow trying to get my car unstuck, and he wasn't the least bit upset at me for the inconvenience. Obviously, it had been an accident, and he saw it just as it was. But there I was, riddled with shame and guilt for being so "careless" as to get stuck in the snow, apologizing over and over.

In my past marriage, I would have been scolded repeatedly, made to feel reckless and irresponsible, like a teenager out for a joyride. Because of my previous psychological abuse, my immediate response was always to apologize for doing something wrong. But Kevin is always there to love me for exactly who I am, seeing the good in me instead. I am so fortunate to know love like this, and I often wonder if this is normal or if I am extra lucky. I don't think there is a way to compare; people's experiences are different because of their pasts. I only hope that I can help our kids understand their worth, but how to also recognize and appreciate the love shown to them.

I did not live a tough life. I grew up privileged and blessed in many ways. I experienced twists and turns along the journey that brought me pain and suffering, sadness and grief, but also so much happiness and joy. The things I went through were difficult, and they've helped shape me. I've realized I was lucky to know that it could've been worse. I have been a part of several social media groups where people have shared going through incredibly difficult things with their partners. Nearly every day I was thankful it wasn't worse than it was for me. It was important to recognize and acknowledge my pain, sadness, and grief because while these experiences might be worse than someone else's, they're not as bad as another's.

Shortly after Scott and I divorced, some of his family members would reach out with their support, offering for me to let them know if there was anything the boys or I needed. Some of our mutual friends did the same. But I never found myself able to ask for their help, always replying "Thank you, I'll let you know."

I had no idea what they were willing to do, and I wasn't capable of putting someone else out for my benefit, even if it were only so I could get to the grocery store alone. I had every other weekend to be able to do that! I couldn't ask for anything specific for fear of embarrassment or yet another letdown. What if I asked if they could watch the boys, but they didn't mean that they'd do that? What if I asked if they could make me a meal, just once, so that I didn't have to cook, but they didn't mean they'd do that either?

Something I've learned post-abuse is that ultra-independence is a coping mechanism and a trauma response. It comes from being let down so many times that you choose to do it yourself, over and over again. I simply could not bring myself to ask for help.

I didn't talk to my family and friends about the things that felt off in my relationship because I was ashamed, and I didn't want them to think less of my husband. But it only hurt me in the long run, and I lost a lot of years fighting a battle I would never win. I didn't think it was my opinion that mattered. I was told that everything was my problem and my job to fix, regardless of what was happening. I wish I had found someone, anyone, to talk to. Once I started opening up to those around me, I was able to see just how bad my relationship was, and how much I needed someone to talk to.

I found myself wanting to talk about the past more and more as time went by, but I also really worried about what other people would think of me when I told my stories. Did I sound like just a bitter divorcee? Did I seem weak? Did talking about it make me seem like I couldn't get over the past and should've just moved on? Except, I had moved on and was in a wonderful part of life but was still attached to him because of our kids.

Talking about Scott and all of the bad things we went through made me feel shameful and embarrassed. "How could you stay with him?" was typically the question I got when telling my story. I was stuck questioning myself, wondering the same. How *could* I have stayed if it were really that bad? And then, *was* it really that bad? I quickly tried to recall stories I could tell to prove to them, and myself, that yes, it was bad. But then it goes back to the beginning – how could I have stayed?

People didn't understand how *knowing* all the "things" didn't make me send him packing, and I couldn't even understand it myself. The truth was, they had no idea what it was like to be brainwashed through years of mental abuse, and that even though the signs were glowing bright neon and screaming at me, I was able to excuse them away. Or they were excused away for me, over and over and over.

I came to peace with the unknown, allowing myself grace in knowing that I will never have the answer to that question. I knew that MY self was strong and independent, capable of making good decisions in the everyday things. I also knew that I wasn't myself with Scott, because I ended up being the woman he wanted me to be, the one that did whatever he asked of me, even if it went against my instincts. Looking back at the young girl that jumped off the runaway hayride without a second thought, just because she knew she might be able to help, I knew I was still that same girl inside. I was a helper by nature, a nurturer, a mother, and a friend. I knew that I tried to be that for Scott, which is exactly how I became his victim.

The history we shared together still haunts me in the most unexpected ways, in the ordinary moments of life. While the continuing connection and communication with him have brought up old feelings and opened wounds that haven't completely healed, sharing my history and what I went through validated my reactions and helped to make sense of where I was now and how I got there. Sharing only bits and pieces of the story didn't do justice to the damage that was done. To truly know me, you needed to know where I'd been.

Kevin and I were watching a "catch the criminal" type show and the victim was being offered a settlement her attorney didn't believe was sufficient. The victim responded that it was enough for her, and she *"just wanted this to be done."* My eyes welled up with tears at that saying, "I just want to be done," because it's exactly what I said years ago when going through the divorce. My attorney at the time told me that I shouldn't settle, and that "just being done" meant it would be extremely difficult to ever get what I deserved in the future, which has proven itself true. I settled for much less than what the state guidelines said I should have received in child support, all because I thought by not fighting him it would all just go away.

I didn't want to fight him, I didn't feel like I deserved to fight, and worse, I didn't believe I was worth it. I didn't know that I was being abused, and I didn't know that I deserved more.

As I was walking through the office at work recently, one of my coworkers said, in passing, "Hey, Jess! How's everything going?"

I turned to face him, cheerfully replying while still walking, "Hey! Everything is great. Hope the same for you!"

I turned back around to continue the journey back to my desk when the biggest smile appeared across my face. I was exactly where I wanted to be, and life was wonderful. I was finally myself, exactly as I wanted to be. I created this world for the three of us, and the choices I'd made after being freed of Scott all led me to this place in my life. All of the everyday decisions, the heavy ones that nearly broke me with the weight of the decision, led me, us, to the life we had today. My children and I were happy and thriving, and the possibilities ahead seemed endless. Life became so comfortable that I picked up hobbies; I became a writer, a birth doula, and a puppy foster. I became the wife and mother I was called to be.

Sharing my story and listening to others tell theirs helped me break through the fog and find my inner truth; I remember what it's like to be me. It hit me at that exact moment that I am *Jess*.

Acknowledgments

Thank you to all the women that have told their stories before me, giving me the courage to find my voice. The stories we have to tell bring us together and teach us that we're not alone.

I've found cheerleaders in unexpected places and could not have done this without their love and support. I am forever grateful for their positivity and encouragement.

To my husband, Kevin, I could never thank you enough for the gift of love you've shared with me. I wish I would have met you sooner to get to do life together from the start, but then we wouldn't be who we are today, and I love us exactly as we are.

About the Author

Jessica lives in a small suburb of Minneapolis with her husband and their four children. In addition to her full-time day job and occasionally moonlighting as a birth doula, she has discovered an interest in writing and hopes to find more time to work on the projects endlessly mulling around in her head.

Made in United States
Orlando, FL
28 March 2022

16228145R00148